Medici Money

PUBLISHED TITLES IN

THE ENTERPRISE SERIES

Ken Auletta
Media Man: Ted Turner's Improbable Empire

Rich Cohen
Machers *and Rockers: Chess Records and the Business of Rock & Roll*

Tim Parks
Medici Money: Banking, Metaphysics, and Art in Fifteenth-Century Florence

George Gilder
The Silicon Eye

FORTHCOMING TITLES

Richard Rayner
California Capitalists

Stanley Bing
Rome: The Rise and Fall of the First Multinational Corporation

James Buchan
Adam Smith

Jagdish Bhagwati
Terrified by Trade

BY TIM PARKS

FICTION

Tongues of Flame

Loving Roger

Home Thoughts

Family Planning

Juggling the Stars

Goodness

Shear

Mimi's Ghost

Europa

Destiny

Judge Savage

Rapids

NONFICTION

Italian Neighbors

An Italian Education

Translating Style

Adultery and Other Diversions

Hell and Back

A Season with Verona

Medici Money

ENTERPRISE

Medici Money

Banking, Metaphysics, and Art in Fifteenth-Century Florence

Tim Parks

Atlas Books

W. W. Norton & Company
New York • London

Printed in the United States of America
First Edition

Manufacturing by The Courier Companies, Inc.
Book design by Chris Welch
Cartography by John McAusland
Production manager: Amanda Morrison

Library of Congress Cataloging-in-Publication Data

Parks, Tim.
Medici money : banking, metaphysics, and art in fifteenth-century Florence / Tim Parks.
p. cm.—(Enterprise)
"Atlas Books."
Includes bibliographical references and index.
ISBN 0-393-05827-1 (hardcover)
1. Banks and banking—Italy—Florence—History. 2. Medici, House of
3. Art, Italian—Italy—Florence.
4. Art, Renaissance—Italy—Florence. 5. Medici, House of—Art patronage.
6. Artists and patrons—Italy—Florence. I. Title. II. Enterprise (New York, N.Y.)
HG3090.F562P37 2005
332.1'0945'09024—dc22
2004030516

Atlas Books, LLC
10 E. 53rd Street, New York, N.Y. 10022

W. W. Norton & Company, Inc.
500 Fifth Avenue, New York, N.Y. 10110
www.wwnorton.com

W. W. Norton & Company Ltd.
Castle House, 75/76 Wells Street, London W1T 3QT

1 2 3 4 5 6 7 8 9 0

Contents

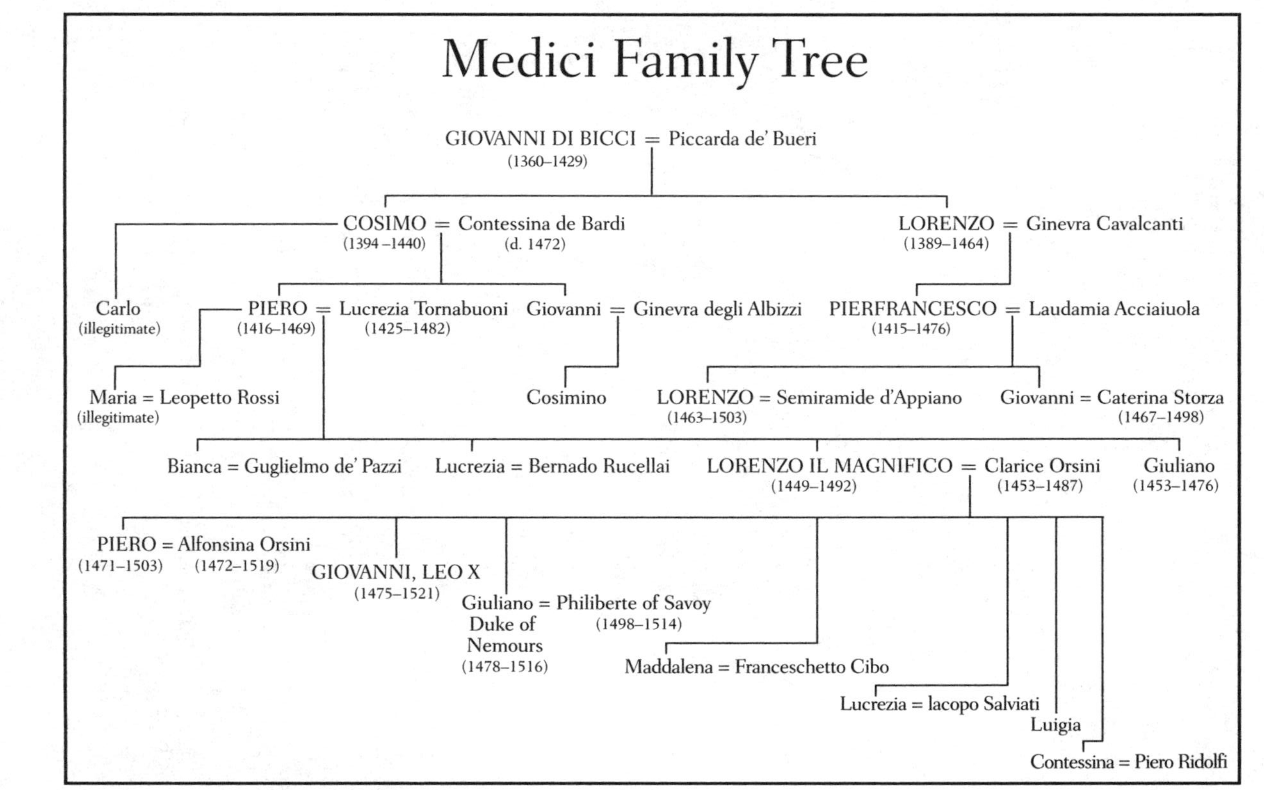
Medici Family Tree
GIOVANNI DI BICCI = Piccarda de' Bueri
(1360–1429)
COSIMO = Contessina de Bardi
(1394 –1440)
(d. 1472)
LORENZO = Ginevra Cavalcanti
(1389–1464)
Carlo
(illegitimate)
PIERO = Lucrezia Tornabuoni
(1416–1469)
(1425–1482)
Giovanni = Ginevra degli Albizzi
PIERFRANCESCO = Laudamia Acciaiuola
(1415–1476)
Maria = Leopetto Rossi
(illegitimate)
Cosimino
LORENZO = Semiramide d'Appiano
(1463–1503)
Giovanni = Caterina Storza
(1467–1498)
Bianca = Guglielmo de' Pazzi
Lucrezia = Bernado Rucellai
LORENZO IL MAGNIFICO = Clarice Orsini
(1449–1492)
(1453–1487)
Giuliano
(1453–1476)
PIERO = Alfonsina Orsini
(1471–1503)
(1472–1519)
GIOVANNI, LEO X
(1475–1521)
Giuliano = Philiberte of Savoy
Duke of
Nemours
(1478–1516)
(1498–1514)
Maddalena = Franceschetto Cibo
Lucrezia = Iacopo Salviati
Luigia
Contessina = Piero Ridolfi

Chronology

1348 The plague kills more than a third of the population of Florence

1378 The revolt of the *ciompi* (woolworkers' rebellion)

1389 Birth of Cosimo de' Medici

1397 Cosimo's father, Giovanni di Bicci, founds the Medici bank in Florence with a branch in Rome

1400 Branch of the Medici bank opens in Naples

1402 Branch of the Medici bank opens in Venice

A Medici wool factory opens in Florence

1406 Florence conquers Pisa

1408 A second Medici wool factory opens in Florence

1410 Baldassarre Cossa elected Pope Giovanni XXIII

1416 Birth of Piero de' Medici (the Gouty)

1420 Death of Baldassarre Cossa; his tomb is commissioned by Cosimo de' Medici

Giovanni di Bicci retires, leaving the bank to his son Cosimo

1424 Milanese army routs the Florentines at Zagonara

1426 Branch of the Medici bank opens in Geneva, later transferred to Lyon

1427 Introduction of the *catasto*, a form of direct taxation

1429 Death of Giovanni di Bicci
War with Milan over Lucca

1433 Branch of the Medici bank opens in Basle
Medici silk factory opens in Florence
September 7, Cosimo de' Medici arrested and exiled

1434 September 29, Cosimo recalled to Florence

1435 Giovanni Benci becomes director of the Medici holding

1436 Branch of the Medici bank opens in Ancona
Dome of the Florence Duomo completed

1436–43 Restoration of the Monastery of San Marco financed and directed by Cosimo de' Medici

1437 Christians in Florence banned from all money-lending practices

1438 Ecumenical conference between leaders of the Byzantine and Roman churches, in Florence

1439 Branch of the Medici bank opens in Bruges

1440 Death of Cosimo's brother, Lorenzo

1442 Branch of the Medici bank opens in Pisa

1443 Closure of the Ancona and Basle branches of the Medici bank

1446 Branches of the Medici bank open in Avignon and London

1449 Birth of Lorenzo de' Medici (the Magnificent)

1450 Francesco Sforza conquers Milan with the help of Cosimo de' Medici

1452 Branch of the Medici bank opens in Milan

1453 Fall of Constantinople

1455 Giovanni Benci, director of the Medici holding, dies and the holding is wound up

1458 Government crisis leads to calling of a *parlamento* and reinforcement of Medici power

1464 Death of Cosimo

Giovanni Tornabuoni becomes director of the Rome branch of the Medici bank

1465 Tommaso Portinari becomes director of the Bruges branch of the Medici bank

Closure of one Medici wool factory

1466 Piero de' Medici calls a *parlamento* and again consolidates Medici power; his son Lorenzo signs a deal with Pope Paul II that gives the bank a monopoly in the alum trade

1469 Death of Piero; his son Lorenzo marries the noble-born Clarice Orsini; Francesco Sassetti becomes sole director of the Medici bank

1471 Florentine army sacks Volterra

1472 Birth of Piero de' Medici (the Fatuous)

1476 Assassination of Galeazzo Maria Sforza, duke of Milan, major client of the Medici bank

1477 Death in battle of Charles, duke of Burgundy (*le Téméraire*), major client of the Medici bank

1478 The conspiracy of the Pazzi. Giuliano de' Medici, Lorenzo's younger brother, assassinated; Lorenzo survives; war with Rome and Naples ensues

Closure of the Milan and Avignon branches of the Medici bank

1479 December, Lorenzo goes alone to Naples to negotiate a peace with King Ferrante

1480 Turks raid Otranto on the southeast coast of Italy and take 10,000 people as slaves

Closure of the Bruges and London branches of the Medici bank and of the Medici silk factory

1481 Closure of the Venice branch of the Medici bank

1485 Lionetto de' Rossi, head of the Lyon branch of the bank, recalled to Florence and arrested for fraudulent bankruptcy

1489 Closure of the Pisa branch of the Medici bank

Lorenzo's second son, Giovanni di Lorenzo de' Medici, later Pope Leo X, becomes a cardinal at the age of thirteen

1490 Death of Francesco Sassetti

Savonarola begins his sermons on the apocalypse in the Monastery of San Marco

1492 Death of Lorenzo de' Medici (the Magnificent)

1494 French invasion; flight of Piero de' Medici (the Fatuous) and collapse of the bank

Medici Money

1

With *Usura* . . .

"*With* usura,"

wrote Ezra Pound,

". . . hath no man a house of good stone
each block cut smooth and well fitting
that design might cover their face."

By *usura*, Pound meant usury, or the lending of money at an interest. Not just an exorbitantly high rate of interest, as in the modern usage of the word *usury*, but any interest at all. He goes on:

"with usura
hath no man a painted paradise on his church wall. . . .
no picture is made to endure nor to live with
but it is made to sell and sell quickly
with usura, sin against nature."

In the 1920s Pound had come to believe, as many still do, that international banking was a source of great evil. He used the Italian word *usura* because it was in Italy that the story had begun. During the thirteenth and fourteenth centuries, a web of credit was spun out across Europe, northward to London, east as far as Constantinople, west to Barcelona, south to Naples and Cyprus. At the heart of this dark web of *usura* lay Florence. But in the same period, and above all in the century that followed, the Tuscan city also produced some of the finest painting and architecture the world has ever seen. Never had stone blocks been cut more smoothly, never were finer paradises painted on church walls. In the Medici family in particular, the two phenomena—modern banking, matchless art—were intimately linked and even mutually sustaining. Pound, it seems, got it wrong. With *usura* we have the Renaissance, no less.

This book is a brief reflection on the Medici of the fifteenth century—their bank; their politics; their marriages, slaves, and mistresses; the conspiracies they survived; the houses they built and the artists they patronized. The attempt throughout will be to suggest how much their story has to tell us about the way we experience the relationship between high culture and credit cards today, how far it informs our continuing suspicions with regard to international finance and its dealings with religion and politics.

The story is complicated. There are five generations to consider. It's important to get the main names and dates and the overall trajectory of the thing firmly in the head from the start.

The bank is founded in 1397 and collapses in 1494. Alas, there will be no centenary party. Giovanni di Bicci de' Medici starts it.

That is: Giovanni, son of Bicci (inexplicable nickname for Averardo), of the Medici family. Born in 1360, Giovanni is responsible for the bank's initial expansion and for establishing a particular Medici style. He keeps his head sensibly down among his flourishing account books before departing this life in 1429. "Stay out of the public eye," he tells his children on his deathbed.

Cosimo di Giovanni de' Medici eventually disobeys that order, which is why he will later be reverently known as Cosimo *Pater Patriae,* Father of His Country. His dates are 1389 to 1464, thus making him the longest lived of our five wealthy men. Having survived brief imprisonment and exile, Cosimo takes the Medici bank to its maximum extension and profitability and moves decisively into politics to the point of more or less running the Florentine Republic. He is a friend to philosophers, architects, and painters; a patron of the arts; and benefactor of major public works. At his death the bank has already entered a decline from which it will never recover.

Piero di Cosimo de' Medici came to be known as Piero *il Gottoso,* or Piero the Gouty. Many male members of the Medici family suffered from gout, a hereditary form of arthritis involving painful and ultimately chronic inflammation of the joints. If Piero was the one singled out for the unhappy nickname, it was simply because he didn't outlive his father long enough to be known for much else. To Piero, however, goes the merit, or blame, of establishing a principle of succession where no succession should have been. Piero was head of the Medici bank by hereditary right, but there was no constitutional reason why he should have taken over from Cosimo as key man in the Florentine state. Frail, bedridden, and bad-tempered, he was nevertheless more determined and effective than his republican enemies. Born in 1416, Piero ran the show for just five years, from 1464 to 1469, before handing over the vast family fortune more or less intact to eldest son Lorenzo in 1469.

Lorenzo was to be known as *Il Magnifico*. So much for keeping out of the public eye. Just twenty when thrust into the limelight, he puts his eggs in other baskets than finance and commerce, allowing the family bank to slide into now-irretrievable decline. Like his father and grandfather, Lorenzo survives a major conspiracy and shows great skills of political manipulation. Unlike them, he aspires to the aristocracy, writes poetry (good poetry), and barely seeks to disguise a vocation for dictatorship. In 1492, aged forty-three, unable, due to the gout, to visit his portly mistress, Lorenzo finally succumbs to a variety of ailments.

Last of the five, Piero di Lorenzo would all too soon be known as Piero the Fatuous. His father's artistic achievements and pretensions to nobility proved less transferable as assets than the vast monetary wealth left by his great-grandfather, now drastically diminished. Born in 1472, Piero possessed but one talent, a flair for the game of Florentine football, as a result of which his two years as head of the family were an unhappy parody of his father's more effective maneuverings. He fled Florence, perhaps unnecessarily, as French troops approached the city in 1494. The family wealth was confiscated, the bank collapsed, and ten years later Piero confirmed his incompetence, or perhaps just bad luck, when he drowned crossing the Garigliano, a river north of Naples.

The trajectory, then, is clear enough. One hundred years. Five generations. A vertiginous rise of fortune—first economic, then political—in the hands of two most able administrators. A brief hinge period presided over by a grumpy, middle-aged man in bed. Then two and a half decades of political ascendancy predicated on a wealth that is rapidly disappearing. Followed by sudden and complete collapse. To which we might add that despite their different characters, our five Medici have certain traits in common beyond the gout. They were all ugly, *Il Magnifico* spectacularly so. And they were avid collectors: of sacred relics and ceremonial armor, of manuscripts, of jewels, of cameos. The collecting habit, with its impulse toward control, order, and possession, is akin to the spheres of both banking and art.

WHEN WE THINK of the period that has come to be known as the Renaissance, we think above all of the fifteenth and early sixteenth centuries; we think of the great art and architecture produced then, from Brunelleschi to Michelangelo; and we are aware of the Medici insofar as they had a relation to that art and those artists. Hence we think of them, and above all of Cosimo and Lorenzo, as living in the heyday of early modern times, before which, with the forward-looking exceptions of Dante, Giotto, and Boccaccio, all is darkness. Thus the myth. Yet there is a sense in which the men we are talking about, and particularly Giovanni di Bicci and Cosimo, must have seen themselves rather as coming *afterward*, of living in the aftermath of something, not the beginning of a golden age.

As bankers they came after the innovations that had given the Italians a virtual monopoly on European finance: after the invention of double-entry bookkeeping, after the advent of the bill of exchange, the letter of credit, and the deposit account. The Medici invented nothing in banking practice, unless perhaps we are to think of the relation between their parent company and subsidiaries as an early form of holding. What's more, all the Medici would have been very aware of coming after banks far larger than their own. The Bardi and Peruzzi banks of the thirteenth and fourteenth centuries had amassed fortunes that the Medici would never equal. Both collapsed in the 1340s, when Edward III of England reneged on huge debts. Giovanni di Bicci de' Medici was in partnership with various men of the Bardi family, employed others, and married his son Cosimo to a Bardi girl. Memories of past glory and a sense of the precariousness of banking wealth must often have been on his mind.

Then, as citizens of Florence, the Medici came after all the upheavals that had made their republic what it was: after the slow collapse of feudal law as the Holy Roman Empire turned its attention northward and lost its grip on a rapidly fragmenting Italy; after the transfer of power, amid endless upheavals, from hereditary lords based in the country to the wealthy classes of the cities; after the formation of a Florentine state with a republican constitution; after the war against papal Rome when the city's government seized and sold Church property until the people rebelled in a frenzy of religious feeling that eventually turned political in the revolt of 1378. This was the so-called *ribellione dei ciompi,* when the city's poor woolworkers tried to oust the mercantile classes as they, the merchants, had ousted the nobles a century before.

"The men left in the government," wrote the sixteenth-century historian Francesco Guicciardini of this revolt, "were mostly plebs, men of the crowd rather than nobles, with Messer Giorgio Scali and Messer Tommaso Strozzi at their head, and with popular support they governed three years in which time they did many ugly things, most of all when, for no crime actually committed, but just to be rid of their enemies, they cut off the heads of Piero di Filippo degli Albizzi, once the most renowned citizen of Florence, and likewise of Messer Donato Barbadori and of many other innocents, until in the end, as is the custom, when the people couldn't put up with it any more, they deserted Messer Giorgio and cut his head off; Messer Tommaso saved his life by fleeing the town and was banned from returning in perpetuity, he and his descendants, and Messer Benedetto degli Alberti, who was one of the first to support them, was sent into exile."

One sentence, two changes of regime, various executions. "*Come è usanza,*" says Guicciardini—"as is the custom." Silvestro de' Medici, the most prominent member of the Medici family and recent head of the Florentine government, had sided with the woolworkers. The family fell into disgrace. Giovanni di Bicci, eighteen at the time, would have seen every reason for keeping his head down, if the alternative was to have it cut off.

But perhaps most of all, the Medici bank came after the great plague of 1348 that wiped out a third of the population of Europe. In 1338, Florence numbered 95,000 inhabitants; in 1427, there were 40,000, which was still about the same as the population of London at the time. "They fell ill daily in their thousands," wrote Boccaccio. "Many dropped dead in the open streets. . . . Such was the multitude of corpses that there was not sufficient consecrated ground for them to be buried in." When it was over, it must have been as if the city had been emptied, the earth lightened of a teeming load. In any event, the rapid growth in trade and population that had characterized the twelfth and thirteenth centuries was now definitely over. Would the world ever be so full and prosperous again? A long period of consolidation and recovery had begun, though often it seemed that no sooner were things returning to normal than the sickness struck once more. In 1363 it carried off Giovanni di Bicci's father when our future banker was still no more than a toddler. "The shops scarce open their doors," wrote Lapo Mazzei in the year 1400, "the judges have left their bench; the seat of government is empty; no man is seen in the courts." People were dying again.

But what was possible for judges and politicians was unforgivable in a young bank clerk. In 1420, despite being a member of the family, Cambio d'Antonio de' Medici was fired for leaving his cashier's post in central Florence to flee yet another bout of the epidemic. Back in 1402, Giovanni di Bicci had been one of the judges who chose which artist would design the bronzes on the doors to the Church of San Giovanni Battista, the Baptistery, the city's oldest church in one of the central piazzas, opposite the still-unfinished *duomo*. The bronzes were commissioned as a votive offering to beg God to spare the city from these endless visitations of the plague. The winning design, by Lorenzo Ghiberti, showed Abraham's sacrifice of his son Isaac.

SO THE MEDICI bankers lived in the aftermath of remarkable innovations and great upheavals. "The people were tired," says

Guicciardini of the years when Giovanni di Bicci was a young man, "and happy to rest." But we can also think of the Medici as coming *before*. For looking back, after the bank was gone, from the turmoil of the sixteenth century, it would seem to historians that Cosimo and Lorenzo de' Medici had belonged to a more self-assured, in some ways even innocent, age. No sooner had Piero the Fatuous fled than Italy was overrun by the French, and then by the Spanish, with the Germans and Swiss doing their best to cash in and complicate matters. It was not unusual for a dozen armies to be on the move across the peninsula, plundering at will. The Medici bank thus came before the sacking of Rome (1527), before the sieges of Naples (1527–28) and Florence (1529–30), before the cruel and suffocating inflexibility of the Counter-Reformation, before Italy lost any practical independence for more than three hundred years. Hence, despite the many wars and occasional torture, the murders and corruption, the interminable vote-rigging and tax evasion that will have to be chronicled in this book, we might nevertheless think of fifteenth-century Florence, the ninety-seven years of the Medici bank, as a quiet parenthesis in the troubled transition from medieval to modern worlds. A time in which usury and art could flourish.

THE PLAGUE KILLED rapidly, but Averardo, or Bicci de' Medici, Giovanni di Bicci's father, had made a will. His wife's dowry of 800 florins (gold) was returned to her. Before his five sons could be considered, a sum of 50 *lire di piccioli* (silver) was set aside for restitution to any lender in whose regard Averardo may have committed the sin of usury. It was a standard formula. The notorious Paduan usurer, Reginaldo degli Scrovegni, had made a much larger restitution some sixty years earlier, and his son Arrigo, to expiate his father's sin and clear the family name, had commissioned Giotto to fresco the Arena Chapel in Padua. One of the frescoes showed sinners burning in hell. The relationship between usury and art is already more ambiguous than Pound would have us believe.

Indeed, as they approached their deathbeds, it seemed that usury was not just *a*, but *the* sin on the minds of wealthy men. Their illegitimate children, the sex they had enjoyed with child slaves from North Africa or the Slavic countries, their greed, gluttony, and general intemperance worried them far less. Or perhaps it was just that usury, unlike other sins, could only, according to Church law, be expiated through *full restitution* of what was sinfully gained. This was difficult if you'd spent the money. The sin loomed large, too, in the minds of those who had never had the wealth to practice it. In the opening story of Boccaccio's *Decameron,* two usurers are terrified that their dying guest, a great and unrepentant sinner, will be refused burial and that because of their profession the local people will chase them out of town or even lynch them, in which case they too will be left unburied. The Lateran Church Council of 1179 denied Christian burial to usurers and the General Church Council of Lyon confirmed the ruling in 1274. "Their bodies should be buried in ditches, together with dogs and cattle," wrote Fra Filippo degli Agazzari. In Piacenza in 1478, when a torrential rainstorm followed the church burial of a usurer, the townsfolk dug up the corpse, paraded it in the streets, performed a mock hanging, then plunged it into the Po.

Why? Why was a transaction that isn't remotely considered a sin or crime today thought so heinous? Especially when other deals—trading in slaves, for example—were not considered sins at all. Is it simply because St. Luke said, "Give, without hoping for gain"? The history books pass rapidly over the matter, or they dwell on those usurers who fleeced the poor with exorbitant rates. But this will not do. When Cosimo de' Medici paid for the restoration of the Monastery of San Marco in return for a papal bull clearing him of all his sins, it certainly wasn't because he had been charging high interest rates to the poor. Cosimo would never have dreamed of dealing with anyone whose credit was not solid, unless perhaps that man were prince or pope.

So before beginning at the beginning—with the moment, that is, in the fall of 1397 when Giovanni di Bicci, together with two partners, registers his bank with the regulating authority in Florence, the so-called Arte di Cambio, or Exchangers' Guild—we must get a grasp of the entirely different mental world in which the man lived, particularly as far as money was concerned, and above all of the profound contradiction between routine banking practices and moral law.

The Exchangers' Guild. "You made a terrible mistake when you joined," one Florentine merchant's partner told him. "Nobody will ever think of you as an honest trader again." Even before the invention of money, there was always something disturbing about the notion of exchange, the idea that one desired thing could always be acquired by the surrender of another. Sulking in his tent, refusing any form of payment for the girl taken from him by Agamemnon so that the king could return another girl to her powerful father without himself losing pleasure or prestige, the hero

Achilles makes the famous remark: "Fat sheep and oxen you can steal; cooking pots and golden-maned horses you can buy; but once it has left the circle of his teeth, the life of a man can be neither replaced, nor stolen, nor bought."

There must be a limit to it, Achilles says. There must be something so sacred as not to be subject to the "art of exchange." But two thousand years later, it was still quite common to buy a girl, or a reduction of one's time in purgatory, or a mercenary army, or a bishopric, or a holy relic, or even a town and all the people in it. Of one pope on his deathbed it was said that he couldn't take the sacraments because, "by God he'd sold them!"

It is King Agamemnon who rules the mad round of exchanges that begins the *Iliad,* and it is the king whose head, in centuries to come, would always appear on coinage. Divinely appointed, the monarch sanctions and governs the practice of exchange, which is to say the economic relationships among the subjects he rules. The process was much speeded up now, of course, for money enables us to sell to one person, store our wealth, then buy from another. We don't have to cast about for that unlikely individual who has exactly what we want and wants exactly what we have. All the same, as long as money is made up of a precious metal that has value *in itself* as a commodity, then nothing fundamental has changed. We sweat to produce, as God told us we must when He threw us out of paradise; we sell our wares for a certain weight of gold or silver or copper, then use that, or part of it, to buy what someone else has sweated to produce. True, some perverse parallels arise: We can now compare the unit cost of a whore with that of a flask of wine, or a copied manuscript, or a prayer for the dead. But everything is still more or less in order and everyone in his place.

Usury alters things. With interest rates, money is no longer a simple and stable metal commodity that just happens to have been chosen as a means of exchange. Projected through time, it multiplies, and this without any toil on the part of the usurer. Everything becomes more fluid. A man can borrow money, buy a loom, sell his wool at a high price, change his station in life. Another man can borrow money, buy the first man's wool, ship it abroad, and sell it at an even higher price. He moves up the social scale. Or if he is unlucky, or foolish, he is ruined. Meanwhile, the usurer, the banker, grows richer and richer. We can't even know how rich, because money can be moved and hidden, and gains on financial transactions are hard to trace. It's pointless to count his sheep and cattle or to measure how much land he owns. Who will make him pay his tithe? Who will make him pay his taxes? Who will persuade him to pay some attention to his soul when life has become so *interesting*? Things are getting out of hand.

Contro natura! thunders the Church—against nature. Usury is unnatural and God punishes it with the plague, warns the preacher Bernardino of Feltre. To defend themselves from the plague, the merchants of Florence pay for an expensive bronze door showing one of the strangest exchanges ever made, or at least proposed: Abraham's sacrifice of Isaac. Ghiberti's doors were so beautiful they were "fit to be the gates of paradise," said Michelangelo. And he was gay. *Contro natura,* thunders the Church. In Dante's hell, sodomites and usurers are punished in the same place, the third ditch of the seventh circle where flakes of burning ash sift for all eternity on an unnatural landscape of scorching sand. The sodomites are forced to exist (how can we say live?) in an unnatural perpetual motion. The usurers are forced to sit unnaturally still, as they did at their accounts. Only their hands move rapidly and unnaturally, as once they moved counting coins or writing bills that have no currency beyond the grave. Their faces are disfigured. Grief bursts from the eyes they ruined over their registers. Unaided by Giotto's frescoes, Reginaldo degli Scrovegni is down there: "He twisted his mouth and stuck out his tongue like an ox that licks its nose." *Contro natura!*

The other inmates of that infernal ditch are the blasphemers. It is unnatural to curse your creator. None of these three sins is considered such today. If a man, today, negotiates a mortgage with a client in the afternoon, has sex with his male lover in the evening, and blurts out, "Christ Almighty," when the alarm starts him from sleep in the morning, we have no difficulty thinking of him as a decent bloke. Or not in the West. In an Islamic state, all three actions are punishable. For the Koran will no more permit the lending of money at an interest than it will allow Salman Rushdie to deride the name of Muhammad, or two consenting males to make love. Usury makes money "copulate," said the theologians, quoting Aristotle. Which is unnatural.

If you still find this hard to grasp, you're in good company. "Go back a little way," Dante's pilgrim poet begs his guide Virgil as they hurry through hell, "to where you told me that usury offends God's goodness, and untie that knot for me." He can't quite see it. Summarizing Thomas Aquinas, Virgil explains that "nature takes its course from heavenly intellect," and that "human toil, as far as it is able, follows nature, as the pupil does his master, so that it is God's grandchild, as it were." In short, God creates work to complete man's nature. Refusing work, the usurer rejects nature, rejects the way God has chosen for him, insults God's grandchild.

Crucially, then, we must imagine a mind that believes that moral codes are based not on the well-being or otherwise of our fellow man—the poor are not mentioned here—but on metaphysics. The distance between believing that lending at an interest is *always* a sin, because *unnatural,* to the modern notion that interest rates are quite normal, but iniquitous when so high that they push a Third World country into poverty, might be one way of measuring the distance between fourteenth-century man and ourselves. That said, however, and granted the good faith of Aquinas and Dante, the sheer violence of the Church's hostility to usury makes it hard to believe that priests and pope didn't have some urgent, worldly interest in the matter. One's "toil," after all, in the medieval world, meant one's station in life—miller, knight, butcher, peasant—which was largely fixed from birth. To refuse one's station was to refuse the fixed order of society in which the Church had a considerable investment, and to throw the world into turmoil.

TURMOIL. "IN OUR change-loving Italy," wrote Enea Silvio Piccolomini, later Pope Pius II, "where nothing stands firm, and where no ancient dynasty exists, a servant can easily become a king." Politically, at the time of Giovanni di Bicci's birth in 1360, the peninsula was on the edge of chaos and had been for some long time. Basically, the twenty or more tiny states of central and northern Italy were kept in a constant ferment of revolution and usurpation by the two opposing and interminably disruptive poles of the Papal States to the south and the Holy Roman Empire to the north, each claiming to be the rightful inheritor of the Roman Empire but neither able to impose its claim. Cities declared independence. Mercenary adventurers carved out little kingdoms for themselves, then went to pope or emperor, or pope *and* emperor, to buy a piece of parchment conferring legitimacy: "As legal overlords of Rimini, or Cremona, or Bologna, we grant you the right to rule there." This in return, of course, for a sum of money, or a share of the taxes. Nobody was impressed. Least of all the next adventurer.

In the country, the nobles' feudal rights depended on recognition of the Holy Roman Emperor as ultimate feudal overlord, so they supported him (the Ghibellines); in the cities, the middle classes, who sought to free themselves from the nobles, tended to side with the pope (the Guelfs). Often it was hard to tell who controlled or legitimately taxed a given territory. Factions abounded. In the cities, the more powerful families built towers to defend themselves against each other. In 1200, Florence had about a hundred such constructions, many more than one hundred and fifty feet high. Even today, Florence doesn't seem large enough for a hundred towers. People threaded the narrow streets between armed camps. Crossing the river Arno at different points meant passing from one family's territory to another. Weapons abounded. The murder rate was frightening. Meanwhile, amid the confusion and in the absence of any recognized authority, two factors came powerfully to the fore: individual charisma and money. "No trace is here visible," writes the great historian Jakob Burckhardt, "of that half religious loyalty by which the legitimate princes of the West were supported; personal popularity is the nearest approach we can find to it. Talent and calculation were the only means of advancement."

But what were talent and calculation without cash? The usurer, the banker, is more dangerous, more powerful, when the traditional structures of society have given way. There is nothing now to obstruct the progress of money. There is nothing more solid and reliable now than the golden florin of Florence, on which, in defiance of ancient hierarchies, no sovereign's head is stamped, just the name *Florentia* on one side and the lily, emblem of the city, on the other. With no king on his coins, the banker is more or less obliged to be a kingmaker himself. He funds this or that side, or is plundered by them. He either controls the fiscal system or he is taxed out of business. Needless to say, the literature of the time was full of attacks on the "lowborn pleb who rises from the depths to great prosperity." Could anyone be more callous, wicked, and proud? "A couple of lengths of red cloth," said the wry Cosimo de' Medici, "and you have your nobleman."

HERE IS A little poem written in the first half of the fourteenth century:

Money makes a man visible
Money makes him seem knowledgeable

Money hides every sin
Money shows what he buys and bought
Money gives him women to enjoy
Money keeps his soul in heaven
Money makes a nobody noble
Money brings his enemy down to earth
Without money a man seems stuck
Since it turns the world and fortune's wheel
And, if you want, it'll send you to paradise.
I reckon the man wise who hoards it up:
Since more than any virtue money
Will ward off melancholy.

Yes, it's a scandal. But nobody is more excited than the person who has discovered a scandal. We sense the poet's horrified enthusiasm. With money you can change your social position, you can have women *and* go to heaven. We must condemn this delirium, but actually we are thriving on it. This is the contradiction behind so much mental activity in the West. We love money and what we imagine it can do and buy, and at the same time we are haunted by a fear as old as Achilles: surely there must be some value that is beyond buying and selling, something beyond the art of exchange. Oh, but not something, please, that tells us that money is *altogether* evil, that the plague that took away my child is God's punishment for my financial transactions.

Behind all this tension lies the conundrum of a religion that began by calling the Christian out of the world to live a life of poverty while waiting for the imminent Second Coming—

"Blessed are the poor for they shall inherit the earth"—but then later and rather confusingly, when the Second Coming never came, became the religion of the establishment and the rich, of people entirely in and of the world. What could this lead to but hypocrisy? Or art?

"It is easier for a camel to pass through the eye of a needle than for the rich man to enter the kingdom of God." Everybody knows that. Yet who was richer than prince and cardinal? Traini's *Last Judgment* in Pisa shows the well-dressed merchants drawing back in dismay as ugly demons cart off the affluent damned. Those men wanted to go to heaven, but they didn't want to stop doing business, if only because, as the humanist Leon Battista Alberti explained, a poor man can never "find it easy to acquire honour and fame." Such is the divided consciousness of the banker in the fourteenth and fifteenth centuries, such the contradiction that over the years will encourage the cultivation of less disturbing nonmonetary values—in philosophy, aesthetics, and love.

WE KNOW THE men from their tax assessments. They were obliged to list their incomes and possessions. Spared that annoyance, the women leave only the value of their dowries. Giovanni di Bicci was not a pleb made good. The Medici had appeared often enough on the parchments that recorded the names of the so-called priors of the city, the nine men who formed the government. But he wasn't wealthy either. He and his four brothers had to share the 800 florins their mother left at her death. Assessed for tax, Giovanni was found liable for a contribution of only 12 florins. But a distant cousin had to pay 220, a very substantial sum. Vieri di Cambio de' Medici ran a bank. However distant, family tended to employ family. Both Giovanni and his elder brother Francesco were taken on, and in 1385, when his own marriage brought a dowry of 500 florins, Giovanni was able to invest and, moving south, become a partner—the executive partner, in fact—in the Rome branch of Vieri's bank. The other things we know about Giovanni's wife are that she was called Piccarda Bueri and that she bore her husband two sons, Cosimo and Lorenzo. But she didn't live with him in Rome.

Rome was a political and economic anomaly. The people of Greenland sold whalebone in Bruges and had the money sent to Rome. The people of Poland shipped furs to Bruges, sold them, and had the money sent to Rome. Or, rather, to the Curia, the pope. The Church demanded its tributes from all over Christendom. While other states collected taxes only from their own citizens and often with great difficulty, Rome was drawing in money from all over Europe. On taking up his benefice, a cardinal, bishop, or abbot was forced to pay the equivalent of the first year's income to Rome. Otherwise, he couldn't take up his lucrative appointment. Money arrived from Scandinavia, from Iceland, from poverty-stricken Scotland. Delayed payment was punishable with excommunication. Don't pay and you go to hell. Announcing an extraordinary jubilee, a papal messenger informs the people of Gand in Flanders that if, during a certain period, they come to mass and leave a generous offering for the war against the Infidel, they will be granted a plenary indulgence. Straight to heaven, no purgatory. The people cough up. Who wouldn't? The messenger counts out the money, coin by coin, with an Italian banker, in Bruges. It is always an Italian banker. Where there is an Italian community, there is a chance of a bank. Where there is no Italian community, there is no bank. In any event, the money is sent to Rome.

One says, "the money is sent," but in fact it was paid out on order to the Curia in Rome, either by a branch of the same bank that had received the money abroad or by a trusted correspondent bank. Actually to travel on horseback or by foot across Europe with money was dangerous. "Beware of rivers in flood," one messenger is warned. "Go armed and in company." So a pilgrim, or priest, or choirmaster traveling to Rome goes first to his nearest bank, in London, Bruges, Cologne, Avignon—except for Constantinople, there are no banks east of the Rhine—buys a letter of credit, travels to Rome, and cashes it on arrival. A little is lost on the exchange rate, a little is paid in bank services, but he cannot be robbed. More than any other organization, it is the Church, then, that, despite its condemnation of many banking practices, needs and stimulates the growth of the international bank. Because the Church is the largest international economic entity. It will be hard for the pope to send to hell the people who collect his taxes and make his grandiose projects possible.

And more than any other organization, it is the Church that aggravates the difficulties of balancing the cash flow around Europe. For how can the banks in Rome continue to pay out Church tributes collected elsewhere if they don't take in any cash? There is already a trade imbalance between Italy and northern Europe. London and Flanders are buying silks, spices, and alum from and through Italy in considerable quantities, but all they have to offer in return are raw English wool, some wall hangings, some Dutch linen. However many of these things they send, it never seems to amount to the value of what they want to buy. Already, then, more money has to be brought into Italy, in coin, than sent out of it. The Rome anomaly makes the situation worse; the papal court is sucking in huge quantities of cash and not sending any back. What arrives in Rome is spent mainly on luxury goods—heavy brocades, silks, artwork, and silverware—and these don't come from Northern Europe.

As far as possible, the bankers, who are also merchants, get around the problem with triangular movements. Florence buys raw wool from the English Cotswolds. The Florentine banks in London can pay the sheep farmers with the money they have taken in for papal tributes. Florence cleans and weaves the wool and sends finished cloth for sale in Rome, where the local branch of the same Florentine banks can now recover some of the cash previously paid out on behalf of their London branches. There are similar triangles through Venice and Barcelona. But the problem is complicated and sometimes gold or silver has to be sent directly to Rome, hidden in a bale of wool perhaps. Or the Germans send ingots from their silver mines under armed guard. It is not very convenient. Fortunately, there were also the so-called discretionary deposits.

In his twelve years working in his cousin's business in Rome, Giovanni di Bicci must have learned everything he needed to know to set up a major bank. He learned how important it was for a bank to have its own branches in the major business centers and how to mix financial and commercial transactions across different countries to keep his capital at work. But most of all, he would have learned how important was the difference between the spirit of the law and its application. When the Church asked for loans from a bank, for example, the bank could not ask for interest in return, because usury was a sin. So in its role as trading company, it would increase the price of the goods it sold to the Church to the tune of the interest it felt it deserved from the loans it had made. All the same, when a bishop, or a cardinal, or the pope himself had money to put in a bank and wanted to play investor rather than borrower, he was eager to get something in return. Though it must not be called an interest. And this, as we shall see, was the discretionary deposit.

There were those priests who denounced sin and screamed foul and promised damnation. And there were those who studied canon law to find the loopholes in it. One suspects an underlying complicity between the two groups, the fundamentalists and the compromisers, as between any permanent enemies. They need each other to become themselves. In any event, both sides put a lot of pressure on words, on the way in which a transaction can be described. So discretionary deposits involve discretion in two senses. The name of the deposit holder is kept secret, hence the arrangement is *discreet*. The holder's return on the money he deposits is at the *discretion* of the banker, and thus is a *gift* and not a contracted interest rate at all, even if it can usually be expected to work out in the region of 8 to 12 percent per annum. Since the banks do not enter into a contractual obligation to make this gift, for that would be usury, and since, on rare occasions when they are losing money, they will not make it, some theologians decide that the arrangement is not usury since there is no certain gain. Others, notably Archbishop (later Saint) Antonino of Florence, consider that since the deposit is made in the *hope* of gain—for the gift is certainly discussed—then this is "mental usury"; the intention is there and the absence of a contract makes no difference. It is a mortal sin.

Despite the secrecy, we know of many famous holders of discretionary deposits. One was Henry Beaufort, bishop of Winchester, half brother of Henry IV. Was his soul at risk? Cardinal Hermann Dwerg, close friend of Pope Martin V, is said to have lived in "a spirit of evangelical poverty," while keeping 4,000 Roman florins in a discretionary deposit and accepting Cosimo de' Medici's annual gifts. Perhaps the cardinal really did live a frugal life. Perhaps he gave generously to the poor.

Occasionally, arguments would develop when a "gift" rashly promised was not forthcoming. The government of Florence, which of course abhorred usury, considered the habit of giving gifts in return for deposits "laudable" and ruled that promises of gifts must be honored. "Contracts were written in obscure and ambiguous language," writes the historian Raymond de Roover, "and so became fertile ground for expensive litigation." The anxiety over mortal sin thus affected not only the actual nature of the financial services offered but also the banking trade's attitude toward language. A transaction would always be recorded, but its true nature was often camouflaged. What matters, the bankers appreciated, is that you must not be *manifestly* in the wrong. Obviously, if a bank failed to produce its gift, the clerical customer took his cash elsewhere.

But why would a cardinal in Rome put his money in a bank that—quite apart from the problem of usury—might, and often did, fail? Why not invest it, sin-free, in property, which was rapidly increasing its value in the city and immediately surrounding countryside, or again in jewels? Alas, it was illegal to transfer the Church's wealth, which included your cardinal's salary, into the private sector. A new pope was within his rights to confiscate the properties of those who had become rich under his predecessor. Land was visible and vulnerable. The papacy changed hands eleven times in the fifteenth century, not counting the periods when there were two or even three popes. "Sell all that you hath and follow me," Christ said, but the rich clerics were eager to leave their wealth to their families, their brothers or nephews or bastard children. Given the availability of new credit tools, money had the advantage that it could be deposited secretly and, in the event of trouble, withdrawn in a foreign city.

So, together with the effects of usury, which dislodged a man from his station in life, something else quite unnatural was happening: A person's wealth was no longer tied to the local community. The actual coinage paid into the bank in Rome by members of Pope Martin V's family might be quickly paid out in the same place against letters of credit, or tributes collected abroad. Meanwhile, in Avignon, Cologne, or Bruges, the Italian banker who had sold those letters of credit, or collected the tributes, could invest the money in a shipment of almonds from Barcelona, or alum from Turkey, which could then be sold on to London. The Church's wealth circulated for fear of a new pope, who, unlike a new king or duke, would come from a different family and very likely a different city than his predecessor, bringing an agenda and an entourage all his own.

Giovanni di Bicci must capitalize on that circulation, on the particular turbulence that seems to occur when money meets metaphysics. In 1393 his elder cousin Vieri de' Medici retired, and Giovanni bought out the Rome branch of the bank. But why, four years later, did he move back to Florence to make the decisive gesture of forming his own bank? And why did Florence become the headquarters of that bank, though it would never begin to equal the profits generated in Rome?

As with the cardinals and their discretionary gifts, the answer has to do with family. How is it, asks an anonymous Genoese writer of the early fourteenth century, that a man will do everything "to acquire power, possessions, lands and goods for the sake of his children, thereby condemning himself to eternal damnation?" It is an interesting question. Just as it's intriguing in the *Divina commedia* how many of Dante's damned seem more concerned with the honor of their family name back in Florence than their eternal torment in hell. Leon Battista Alberti answers the question in *Della famiglia,* written in the 1430s. Since the family is the social unit par excellence, Alberti says, any attitude or investment that benefits your family or serves to increase its honor is acceptable, for this is the determining purpose of life.

In short—though Alberti would never have put it like this—if making money has become an addiction, nevertheless family allows you to think of your moneymaking as a means to an end. Family offers a value, a reason for living at once more noble than mere accumulation, and more immediate than the pleasures of

Giovanni di Bicci de' Medici, as portrayed by Bronzino. The founder of the bank, Giovanni warned his children to "stay out of the public eye," as if he had already appreciated the dangers of mixing politics and finance.

paradise. And while wealth in money terms might now be cut free from place, family could not. The Medici family was deeply rooted in Florence. There was property and a network of old alliances. If Giovanni had left his wife and children back in Florence when he went to Rome, it was because he himself always meant to return. Doing so, he would cease to be at the outpost of a network and place himself firmly at its center. He would once again exercise his political rights as a Florentine citizen and become a full and feared member of society, something that could never have happened in Rome. The injunction, "keep away from the public eye," did not necessarily mean, "deny yourself political power." In fact, one might keep out of the public eye precisely in order to accumulate power. Added to which, unlike the Romans, the Tuscans had a long tradition in running international banks, which were the key to making money, from Rome.

2

The Art of Exchange

"Bank," Italian *banco* (later *banca*): a bench, table, or board, something to write on, to count over, to divide two people engaged in a transaction. That was all the furniture you needed. For some people a bank was just a *tavola,* a table. The Medici have their table in via Porta Rossa, they would say. Some things passed above board, and some below.

Since the bankers often did business together, they set up these tables in the same neighborhood—Orsanmichele, around what is now the Mercato Nuovo. There were about seventy all told. Halfway between Ponte Vecchio and the still-unfinished *duomo,* under shaded porticoes, or behind the massive doors of the *palazzi,* the moneymen stood or sat, wrapped in their long red gowns, bags of coins at their sides.

Above the table, on a green cloth, lay the big official ledger. The Exchangers' Guild rules that every transaction must be written down. The banker has ink-stained fingers. "In the name of God and of profit!" the book begins. Or: "In the name of the Holy Trinity and of all the saints and angels of Paradise." Every angle was covered.

The written check existed but was not the norm. Too risky. Every transaction must be ordered orally by the client in person and written down in his presence, with Roman numerals, in careful columns, because these are more difficult to alter. No sooner does money project itself through time and space than it generates vast quantities of writing. It becomes a thing of the mind, fluid and fickle. Write it down!

The merchant watches patiently as the quill scratches out his entry. Literacy is on the increase. The silence of men concentrating on numbers, dates, is invaded by the clatter of carts in the street, the cackle of caged poultry, the occasional shouts of the town crier. Downtown Florence is a busy place. In the Mercato Vecchio, a couple of hundred yards away, bales of silk and barrels of grain are changing hands. The bakers shovel their bread from the communal oven.

Once completed, the entry is read out loud. Any member of the Exchangers' Guild found to have destroyed or altered his accounts is expelled without appeal. Whereas the Church's rules may be open to debate, these are not. And when a banker dies leaving no one to carry on the business, his ledgers are held by the guild in a chest with three locks so that three officials, each with his own key, must all be present before the accounts can be consulted. Money, like mysticism, thrives on ritual.

Not all banks are in the same league. Where a red cloth hangs from the arch of the door, that's a pawnbroker making modest loans in return for a declared interest rate and against the security of some object that can be resold if he is not repaid: a pair of wooden clogs, perhaps, decorated with embroidered cloth; or a wedding chest painted with biblical scenes; or the detachable brocaded sleeves for a lady's dress. Such items are desirable. It is not a throwaway society.

Making no attempt to hide his profit, the pawnbroker, whether Christian or Jew, is a "manifest usurer" and so cannot belong to the Exchangers' Guild and cannot be given a license to trade. But he can be fined. Or rather, *they* can. For this "detestable sin," as the city's government deems it, a fine of 2,000 florins a year is imposed on all the Florentine pawnbrokers as a group. Payment exempts them from any further tax or punishment. The theologians can debate whether this arrangement amounts to granting a license or not. Once again, language is used to perpetuate a contradiction rather than offer clarity. Is usury forbidden or isn't it? Could it be that a manifest usurer is actually more honest than the nonmanifest variety? Deplored and indispensable, the pawnbroker, like the prostitute, continues to trade. Only after 1437 would Christians in Florence be banned from the business altogether. This eliminated a contradiction—if the Church says you mustn't, then you really mustn't—and focused all the poorer community's resentment on the Jews.

Unlike the pawnbrokers, the *banche a minuto* were regularly signed-up members of the guild. These were small and strictly local banks with three main functions: They sold jewels, accepting payment by installment; they held tied deposits, on which they handed out annual "gifts" amounting to 9 or 10 percent; and they changed silver *piccioli* into gold florins, and vice versa.

What's that? Here, before tackling the *banca grossa*—the international bank, the merchant bank, the Medici kind of bank—we must get a grip on the currency. Or currencies.

The purpose of any currency, you would have thought, is to offer a unit of wealth that, when multiplied or divided, will buy anything for sale within a given geographical area. This is at once the wonder and danger of money, that in different amounts it can be made equivalent to almost anything. Hence we have copper coins that can be added up to make silver coins, silver that can be added up to make gold, or, in our day, the banknote, one dollar, five, ten, twenty, a hundred.

Not so in fifteenth-century Florence. Your silver coin, the *picciolo,* could not be added up to make a golden florin. They were separate currencies. The logic of this was that since the two coins were actually made of precious metals—indeed their worth depended on the intrinsic value of each mineral—the relationship between them could no more be fixed than the relationship between apples and oranges. *Piccioli* could only be changed into florins by the bank at the going rate for changing silver into gold.

Thus the reasoning. The reality was that into the very element that potentially frees us from class—the element that allows the hateful parvenu to pile up wealth and act as if his peasant family were as noble as mine—a radical divide was established. The *picciolo* was the currency of the poor, the salary of the worker, the price of a piece of bread. Luxury goods, wholesaling, international trade, these were the exclusive realm of the golden florin. By law. It was a situation not unlike that in the communist bloc some years ago where the rich and powerful used the dollar and the masses the *zloty* or *rouble*. A man who dealt in *piccioli* had a long way to go.

Across the banker's green table you could make the move from one world to another, from silver to gold, modesty to riches. At the price of a small commission. Needless to say, the poor man's money tended to be worth less and less. In 1252, when the florin was first minted, it could be bought with a *lira* of *piccioli*, which is to say 20 *piccioli*. Around 1500, you needed 7 *lire* of *piccioli*—i.e., 140. This was partly because the merchant who belonged to the Arte di Calimala (the Merchants' Guild), the silk manufacturer who belonged to the Arte di Por San Maria (the Clothmakers' Guild) earned in florins but paid salaries in *piccioli*. When profits were down, they encouraged the mint, which was controlled by the government, which in turn was formed mainly of men from these powerful guilds, to reduce the silver content in the *picciolo*. That way it would take fewer florins to pay the same salaries in *piccioli* to the unsuspecting poor. Archbishop Antonino condemned this practice. The archbishop was well loved for his constant work to improve the lot of the poor. He even went around personally to put bread in the hands of dying plague victims. But nobody was ever excommunicated for fiddling the currency, as they were when a debt to the pope wasn't paid. Nor was anyone publicly whipped, or put in the stocks, as when a silkworker stole some of the material she was weaving.

So separate currencies guaranteed that despite all the social turmoil, some salutary hierarchical distinctions were maintained. Assessed for tax in 1457, 82 percent of Florentines paid less than a florin and 30 percent nothing at all, because destitute. This monetary apartheid, however, came at the price of some serious accounting problems. Dealing only in florins, Giovanni di Bicci's bank could use the double-entry system, with debits and credits on opposite pages, Venetian style. But when the family opened a wool-manufacturing business, more primitive methods had to be adopted. Who was to say what the exact relationship between purchases, earnings, and salaries was, when one side of the company dealt in florins, the other in *piccioli*? In any event, when business was bad and neither gold nor silver was to be had, the workers were obliged to accept payment in woolen cloth, which they hated, and which messed up the books even further, though it did benefit the pawnbrokers, who had a habit of turning cloth into cash at rates that suited them. However potentially evil money may be, the mind does long for the clarity and convenience of the transferable unit of value.

HOW MUCH WAS the florin worth? A slave girl, or a mule, could be bought for 50 florins. To purchase the *piccioli* that would pay a maid's wages for a year might cost 10 florins. Thirty-five florins would pay a year's rent for a small townhouse with garden, or for the Medici's banking premises on the corner of via Porta Rossa and via dell'Arte della Lana. Twenty florins would fresco the courtyard of a *palazzo* costing 1,000 to build, or pay an apprentice boy at the bank for a year, while a barrel of wine would come in at just a *lira de piccioli* and a visit to the astrologer half that. "Don't trade in wine," Cosimo would tell his branch managers, "it's not worth it." But he regularly consulted astrologers. Money and magic go together. A leek cost one *picciolo* and an arm's length of cheap cloth 9 *piccioli,* while the same length of gorgeous white damask would set you back 2½ florins, about twenty-five times the price, depending on the exchange rate. In general, luxury goods were expensive—the rich needed their florins—while the staples were cheap, so that, assuming they had been paid, the laborers could get by on their *piccioli*. But the city's many wool- and silkworkers were on piece rates and demand was not steady. In hard times, you might be better off as a slave at a rich man's table.

All the same, despite low wages and separate currencies, the scandal of moneymaking continued, for money will not stay still and the poor are rarely happy with their lot. So if you did manage to lay in a little store of cash, there were laws to prevent you from upsetting others by showing it off. No meal with more than two courses for the common classes. No more than a certain number of guests at any given meal. No clothes with more than one color, unless you are a knight or his lady. Or a magistrate, perhaps. Or a doctor. No fine materials for children. No soft leather soles on your white linen socks. No fur collars. No buttons on women's clothes except between wrist and elbow, and for maids, none at all. For maids, in fact, no fancy headdress and no high heels, just kerchief and clogs.

The plebs were thus prevented from spending themselves into poverty. A sensible thing surely. Such legislation keeps the natural order natural. Money can't cause trouble if people aren't allowed to use it. Was the inspiration behind the laws just a touch misogynist? No doubt the threat of being birched naked through the streets guaranteed a certain frisson when a girl broke the rules and sewed a silver button at her breast.

Sporadically enforced, because in the end bad for business (this was a town that specialized in the production of luxury clothing), the so-called sumptuary laws kept everyone hyperconscious of status. Spying on your neighbors is exciting. Fashions were constantly changing to beat the letter of the law. If such and such a material was banned, then a new one was invented. As in the area of finance, repression proved a great stimulus for creativity, to the detriment of plain speech. This sleeve may look like samite, *signora,* says the dressmaker, but technically speaking it's something else. A French invention. Not covered by the legislation. This may look like a row of buttons, but as you see there are no buttonholes, so strictly speaking they are studs.

The legislators worked hard to keep ahead of the game. "Clarification about pearls," announces one new law. "Clarification about buttons." "Clarification about the wearing of chains." But, as for the theologians pondering new financial instruments, the task was endless. "How can we ever curb the disgraceful bestiality of our women?" asks one despairing member of the government. Fashion police were appointed to roam the streets and finger ladies' clothes. The Officers of the Night, they were called. "Oh, but the collar is suckling, sir, not ermine!" "And what's suckling?" "An animal, sir." Meanwhile, Giovanni di Bicci and his two sons wore sober cloaks. They hadn't yet tackled the problem of how to make their wealth manifest. For the moment, envy was a weed best left unwatered. One of Cosimo's favorite sayings.

Because the florin was worth a great deal and could not be broken down into smaller coins (otherwise the poor would have begun to use it), bankers found it necessary to invent an accounting currency, so that wholesale prices and discretionary gifts could be calculated in fractions of florins. So the *lira a fiorino* must rapidly be mentioned. This was worth twenty twenty-ninths of a florin (yes, $^{20}/_{29}$) and each *lira a fiorino* could be divided into 20 *soldi a fiorino,* which in turn could be divided into 12 *denari a fiorino*. Hence there were 348 *denari* or 29 *soldi* in a gold florin, though of course there were no such coins as the *soldo* and the *denaro*. Who says money and imagination don't go together? To help them do their sums, each banker was equipped with an abacus. Perhaps not surprisingly, they couldn't always get their books to balance, despite a thorough knowledge of the rules of double entry. "May God save us in future from greater mistakes," writes one Medici branch director to the head office, unable to find out where he has gone wrong.

How mysterious these imaginary currencies must have seemed to the uninitiated in a world where everything but the Holy Ghost was visible. Technology had not yet removed the ordinary things of life from view. Piss did not stream into clear water to be sucked away beneath gleaming porcelain. Shit steamed in the pan. If you were a florin kind of person, you could pay a *picciolo* person to take it away for you and empty it elsewhere. In a back alley, perhaps. The plague victim did not die in starched sheets, nor was his agony alleviated by analgesics. Where there was a perfume, that was because an unpleasant smell was lurking beneath. Your mortality was ever present. People died young.

But there were good smells, too. Packaging hadn't stretched its shiny film over meats and vegetables, wools and silks. Since windows of oiled cotton didn't let in much light, the weavers took their looms to the door. The cobblers and saddlers worked their goods in the street. By the Gora Canal, men are washing the raw wool that will soon be on someone's back. The fishermen come in from the country with carp in their buckets. They pass the barber shaving customers at a corner. The apothecary is grinding nutmeg for cough relief. There are onions for your piles. Everything is present. Every task is clear. That is the natural order: people getting by with the sweat of their brows, as God commanded. Even the feudal lord in the country keeps an army and hires it out, governs his lands. That is understandable. Even the priest helps your soul to paradise when the solid flesh finally melts and the breath rattles its last. Who would deny the need for a church? But what on earth are these bankers doing counting in coins that don't exist?

RETURNING TO FLORENCE in 1397, Giovanni di Bicci put 5,500 florins into his new bank. Already he had at least doubled the 5,000 his wife brought him eight years earlier. The other partners were Benedetto di Lippaccio of the famous Bardi family, who was already working with Giovanni in Rome—he brought 2,000 florins—and Gentile di Baldassarre Boni, who added 2,500 to make 10,000 in all. Things got off to a bad start. Gentile Boni pulled out after a few months, taking his capital with him. Mistake. While his ex-partners grew rich, he would end his life in a debtors' prison. Giovanni increased his capital contribution to 6,000 florins to bring the total to 8,000, and after paying rent and salaries and setting aside a reserve for bad debts, the company got through its first eighteen months with a modest profit of 1,200 florins, 10 percent annually, on the nail.

Over the next twenty-three years, up to Giovanni's retirement in 1420, the bank as a whole would make total profits of 152,820 florins (6,644 p.a.). Giovanni took three-quarters. From 1420 to the next reorganization in 1435, during which time the partners were Cosimo de' Medici, his brother Lorenzo, and Benedetto de' Bardi's brother Ilarione, profits were 186,382 florins (11,648 p.a.). The Medici took two-thirds. From 1435 to 1450, when the bank was in its heyday, profits were 290,791 florins (19,386 p.a.). The Medici, with new partners now, took 70 percent. Keep firmly in mind that a respectable *palazzo* would cost only a thousand to build and that the vast majority of the populace were too poor to pay so much as a single florin in tax.

How was this done, given that it was forbidden to lend money at an interest? Like all major banks at the time, the Medici were merchants as well as bankers. They would procure goods abroad for rich clients: tapestries, wall hangings, painted panels, chandeliers, manuscript books, silverware, jewels, slaves. They would speculate, buying shiploads of alum (for the textile business) or wool or spices or almonds or silks, moving them from southern to northern Europe, or vice versa, and selling at a higher price.

There was a risk involved. A buyer wouldn't give you a florin until he'd seen the goods. Demand and prices swung alarmingly, depending on how many merchants had sensed a particular gap in the market. A lot could happen in the months it took a Florentine galley to sail and row west from Pisa across the Mediterranean, through the Strait of Gibraltar into the Atlantic, then north up the Portuguese, Spanish, and French coasts, east to Bruges, and finally across the English Channel to London. Perhaps there were no customers by the time you arrived. Ships could sink, especially the newer, so-called round ships, which were all sail. The bellying sail became an image of chance. The goddess of fortune stood blindfolded at the mast. In short, the cargoes had to be insured. Groups of banks would get together to underwrite eventual losses. "May God and fortune be our aid," implored the shipping documents.

The merchants reacted to risk by spreading investments over a wide variety of goods and customers. Every bank had its warehouse. Along with the raw silks and wool and linen, an inventory in the Medici's Florence warehouse in 1427 lists "*un corno di liochorno*"—the horn of a narwhal or rhinoceros. In 1489 a giraffe died on its way to the duchess of Bourbon. Who would deny such enterprising men their profits? Yet the accounts show that trade accounted for only a modest percentage of the bank's profits. By trade alone, the Medici would not have become fabulously wealthy. How did they do it?

By the art of exchange.

A man comes to our green-covered table in Florence, in Rome, or after 1400 it might be Naples, after 1402 Venice. He wants money. He is a merchant most probably, in any event creditworthy, otherwise we won't deal with him. He wants, say, 1,000 florins. Why should we give it to him, if we can't ask for interest? He isn't a friend or relative. He offers us an exchange deal. He will take the florins and repay us in pounds sterling, in London. No harm in that. The cashier consults with the branch director. Depending on the conditions of his contract, the director may have to write to the head office. But eventually the money is brought from the strongbox. In return, the merchant—or he might be a magistrate—writes us a *cambiale,* or bill of exchange:

In the year of our Lord 1417 June 15, in Florence,
1000 Florins.

Pay *as is the custom* 1000 florins at 40 pence to the florin to whoever is appointed by Giovanni de' Medici and partners in London. May Christ protect you.

He signs the note. But it is not the signature that is important. It is *all* the handwriting on the bill. Whoever is to pay out the cash in London will have an example of that handwriting and match it carefully with the bill. In general, all the branches of the Medici banks and all those acting as correspondents for them will have examples of the handwriting of all the managers who have the authority to order payments.

When and how will our client repay us? The "how" is easy. His agent in London will pay our correspondent. In sterling. Or rather our correspondent in London will go to his agent's office, probably a bank, and hence Italian, someone we know, to demand payment on the appropriate day.

What day? Well, how long does it take to get from Florence to London? How long is a piece of string? It depends how you travel. Overland or galley, in haste or at leisure. The English Channel can be rough, never mind the Bay of Biscay. Fortunately, the Exchangers' Guild has laid down what is the maximum time that a whole range of journeys from one financial center to another can require. Florence to Bruges, sixty days. Florence to Venice, ten days. Florence to Avignon, thirty days. Florence to Barcelona, sixty days. The time to London is ninety days, or three months. That is what the bill means when it says, "as is the custom." It is referring, very discreetly, to the time between the payment in florins and the repayment in sterling. If our man has taken his florins on June 15, the custom is that the pounds should be ours on September 13. We could agree on an earlier day if we wanted. But we can't postpone it, because in that case the whole thing would begin to look rather like a loan and not an exchange deal at all.

In the early days, the Medici bank didn't have a branch in London, but they had trusted correspondents there. Often the bank's allies abroad were neighbors, perhaps rivals at home. It is easier to feel solidarity abroad. Copies of the bill of exchange are made and the original is sent to Totto Machiavelli and Ubertino de' Bardi and company in London. The names are always familiar. The banks run their own courier system. The day comes. In return for a small commission, our correspondent sends a clerk to our client's agent, who, again in return for a commission, pays out the pounds and pennies. The exchange deal has taken place. How can anybody object?

But where is the return for us, the bank? The bank—this is the official position of all those involved—speculates on the shifting exchange rate in the hope that when it gets its pounds changed back into florins, they will be worth more than the 1,000 florins originally lent. But a child could see that in that case, the bank would always be hesitant to accept a deal. There would be periods when the florin was rising and no one would give you the money because it would doubtless be worth less when it came back in pounds. "*Pro e danno di cambio,*" reads the entry in the Medici bank's accounts. Profit and loss from exchanges. Out of sixty-seven exchanges for which we have records among London, Bruges, and Venice, only one resulted in a loss for the banker, while the remaining sixty-six saw him making gains that range between 7.7 and 28.8 percent. How?

The exchange rates are fixed daily, Sundays and holidays excluded, by paid bill brokers meeting together with merchants and bankers in the open street. In rainy Lombard Street in London. On the breezy Rialto in Venice. They don't meet in anyone's premises, since that would be an acknowledgment of that person's supremacy. They consider trends in trade. They are aware of currencies whose coins are subject to a little trimming. Any member of the Exchangers' Guild caught trimming his coins is liable to immediate expulsion! And the same goes for anyone passing on trimmed coins. Directly upon minting, the florin is sealed in leather bags, the so-called *fiorino di suggello,* or sealed florin. This to avoid trimming. But everybody knows that some people open the bags, replace the coins or trim them down, then reseal them. The florin is under observation. It is losing value against the Venetian ducat, and the Roman florin, not to mention Geneva's golden mark. These experts know which mints are reducing or increasing the gold content, which currencies are silver based and which gold. Milan's silver imperial just goes down and down. They know which governments are trying to intervene in the market, which way the speculators are moving. They get together daily and fix the rates as honestly as they can. Why, then, is the florin always worth about 4 pence more in Florence than it is in London?

Keep your eye on the ball. Our customer takes his 1,000 florins in Florence, where the florin is declared to be worth 40 English pence. The bill of exchange is written out at that rate. He instructs his agent in London to pay out in three months' time. He does so. Our correspondent collects 40,000 pence (or £166 1s. 6d.). We, the bank, then instruct the correspondent to look for—and let us assume he finds—a local client, in London, wishing for a loan of the same amount and offering to pay it back in florins in, of course, three months' time, the time it takes (officially!) to go from London to Florence. Perhaps he is a merchant buying a consignment of wool, speculating that when it arrives in Italy he can sell it for far more than what he paid for it in the Cotswolds.

So another bill of exchange is written out. But, even disregarding temporal fluctuations, the exchange rate is different in London. Here the pound is worth more. Here it will only take 36 pence to buy a florin. So the bill is written out at that exchange rate: Pay *as is the custom* £166 1s. 6d. (40,000 pence) in florins at a rate of 36 pence to the florin. And three months later, if all goes according to plan, we collect 40,000/36 = 1,111 florins. In six months we, the original lending bank, have made 11 percent, which is to say, an annual interest rate of 22 percent.

The Medici made hundreds of these deals. Basically, the trick is that the currency quoted as a unit is always worth a small percentage more in the country of issue. As far as Florence and northern Europe are concerned, the difference in the two exchange rates, which determines the banker's profit, tends to be greatest in early spring, just before the Florentine galleys set out from Pisa for their long trip to Bruges. Because this is when demand for credit to finance trade is highest. It then narrows in the summertime. Manuals are written to help merchants and bankers get their minds around the system. Who needs interest rates?

But was it usury or wasn't it? The theologians pondered. The bankers consulted them. No one wants to go to hell. Was it a loan with an interest rate, or was it an exchange deal? Remember, if currency rates changed drastically during the period of the transaction, then even the institutional difference between currency rates in different countries would not be enough to save the banker from a loss, or at least a very low profit. Conversely, the lender could find himself paying a very high price for his loan if rates went further against him than they already were—if the pound, for example, rose vertiginously while those galleys were fighting their way up the Portuguese coast. As long as the geographical distance was maintained, the theologians decided, as long as there was a real exchange of currencies, as long as there was an element of risk, it wasn't usury.

But to retain their credibility, the doctors of divinity cried a very loud foul at the so-called *cambio secco,* or dry exchange. In this kind of deal, when the bill of exchange became due in the foreign currency—say, sterling—the client did not pay up, but, after consulting the going currency rate, bought another bill for the exact amount owed. It is as if the first and second customers of the legitimate exchange described above, the man borrowing florins and the man borrowing pounds, were in fact the same person. This second bill then became due in the place where the first bill was issued—say, Florence—in florins, after the required period and at the new exchange rate. In this way, the period of the loan was doubled while the parties involved avoided actually using a foreign currency at all, although the element of speculation on rates, and hence of risk, was still there, since the exchange rates in London on the day in question were observed and a bill of exchange was written up. Hence, to be perfectly logical, there was no reason to say that this was any more or less usury than the regular bill of exchange. All the same, it was vigorously condemned by theologians because now it had become obvious that what the client really wanted was a loan, and not an exchange deal. Motivation is important. In 1429 the government of Florence banned the practice. It was clearly no more than a scam for usury. "To trade in *licit* exchanges." Such was the declared purpose of the Medici bank. Yet it frequently dealt in "dry exchanges." In 1435, when Cosimo took a dominant position in Florentine politics, the law forbidding such exchanges was swiftly revoked.

THIS THEN WAS the state of play: Usury was abominable but people needed loans and bankers a return for giving them. The complex system of differing exchange rates, possible only because of the time it took to travel from one financial center to another, provided an ambiguous territory that kept trade moving and many in a constant state of anxiety as to the destination of their eternal souls. Some merchants steered clear of the whole business, convinced it was a sin. Some less scrupulous operators were happy about the Church's position because it scared off the squeamish and reduced the competition. The practical effect was that long-term loans became difficult, because a bill of exchange must always be paid in no more than the time officially required to reach one of the major European centers. Capital investment suffered. The bank became anchored to trade rather than manufacturing and was forced to become international, when otherwise it might well have stayed local. Loans were more expensive than they need have been, and highly speculative. "Exchange is a bird of passage," warns one banking manual, "grab it while you can, it won't be back!" Above all, there was constant tension between what people said they were doing, what they knew they were really doing, and what they knew they were supposed not to be doing. Meantime, every letter between banks on whatever matter always carried an *avviso,* a warning, or announcement, of currency rates on that day. Already information was of the essence. *Stare sugli avvisi,* to be on your guard, came to mean to deal in bills of exchange. On your guard! Such is the special excitement of dealing in money: am I winning or losing, am I going to heaven or hell?

One of the ways Giovanni di Bicci had always been on his guard was in his determination to have close relations with the Church, the ultimate source of capital: spiritual, political, and monetary. While in Rome, he had met the extrovert Neapolitan priest Baldassarre Cossa. Was it Giovanni di Bicci who funded the man's purchase of a cardinal's hat in 1402? It's not clear. In any event, Cossa took to addressing the banker as "My most dear friend," in his many letters.

In 1410, Cossa was elected pope and became Giovanni XXIII (but not, of course, *the* Giovanni XXIII of the Second Vatican Council—of which more later). Down in Rome, Ilarione di Lippaccio de' Bardi, brother of Giovanni di Bicci's partner Benedetto and now director of the Medici bank's Rome branch, immediately became Depositary of the Papal Chamber. Which is to say, the Medici bank in Rome now held the pope's cash, collected his vast incomes, paid out his vast expenditures. They lent him money for war on Naples and they lent him more money to pay the reparations when he lost the war. Indispensable—and friendly too!—the bank began to suggest whom the pope might appoint to this or that bishopric, then collected the fees due when the appointee took up his position. Obviously, the bankers only proposed candidates who were in a position to pay promptly. Throughout Giovanni di Bicci's life, and much of Cosimo's, more than 50 percent of the Medici bank's profits came from Rome.

To invest that holy income (in ambiguous bills of exchange), the bank had already opened two new branches in major trading centers, Naples and Venice. The relationship of these branches to each other and to the central office in Florence was to be crucial. The Bardi and Peruzzi banks that had preceded the Medici collapsed in part because of bad debts to foreign monarchs, but in part also because there was no juridical distinction between its operations in different countries. The bank as a whole was liable for the debts of each of its outlets. If money is allowed to flow without restraint, a sudden movement will tip the boat. Worse, in order to fund such a huge international operation, the Peruzzi in particular had brought a large number of partners into what was a single, monolithic organization, with the result that eventually they lost overall control. When money began to leak drastically from one or another branch and the ship listed, the various partners began to argue. It was hard to steer to a safe haven.

Giovanni di Bicci resolved these difficulties with a simple structural correction, and in doing so revealed at once what was to be the genius of the Medici family: its manipulation of people within organizational structures—first financial, but later social and political too. Each branch was to be a separate company. The shareholders were: the branch director, to the tune of something between 10 and 40 percent, and then the Medici bank for the rest. *Not* the Medici family personally, and not the Florence branch, which had the same status as the other branches, but rather a separate holding company located in a separate office in Florence. In this way, a large number of capital-bearing partners could be brought in—one or two in each branch and one or two more important figures in the holding—without the Medici themselves ever losing control of either the parts or the whole.

A branch director would receive expenses and a considerably larger percentage of the profits than his own share of the investment would appear to warrant. This to motivate him. In return, he was obliged under contract to live in his branch's city and to observe the rules enforced by the holding company: Don't lend more than 300 florins to cardinals; to courtiers no more than 200; don't give credit to any Roman merchant, unreliable; nor to feudal barons, not even if they give you security (barons are a law unto themselves); and never, never lend money to Germans, since their courts won't respect your claim if, or rather when, things go wrong.

Between cashiers, letter writers, messenger boys, and managers, there were about four to eight people in each branch—all working, eating, and sleeping in the same building, sharing the same one or two servants, slaves, and horses. The holding company in Florence was responsible for all hirings and firings. And salaries. Otherwise, who knows what complicity might arise between a branch director and his staff in a distant city? In addition to the official ledgers, there was also a "secret book" in which the director wrote down such things as the discretionary deposits of clients who wished to remain anonymous. And salaries. No one must know another's salary. There must be no opportunity for private gripes and local conspiracies against the head office. The secret book was made of parchment, not paper, to last longer, and kept under lock and key, often in the director's bedroom. Once a year it would be taken to Florence for discussion. Above all, each branch dealt with the others as with any other company. Each was part of a whole, but simultaneously in competition; each running its own show, but under observation. Thus the Medici learned the techniques they would later apply in the political sphere: Divide, be reasonably generous, and rule.

Yet at once it became clear that however sophisticated the structure you formulated, the choice of staff would always be crucial. To make money, you need astute men and honest. And healthy. No sooner had Castellano di Tommaso Frescobaldi been appointed, in 1400, to run things in Naples than he fell sick and died. Good management can do nothing about the plague. Neri di Cipriano of the once-noble Tornaquinci family became the first director in Venice, in 1402, and immediately broke contract by lending money to Germans. Even Poles! He never recovered it. Faking the books, both manifest and secret, he invented a first-year profit and borrowed at 8 percent to have further capital, which he went on losing. Since the Medici did not routinely send inspectors to their various branches, it was three years before the now-considerable reversal of nearly 14,000 florins was discovered. Dealing in money is so exciting because its liquid nature makes the losses as great and as swift as the profits. The medieval wheel of fortune has speeded up. Everything is levered and intensified. Condemned by the Venice courts, Tornaquinci surrendered his belongings and fled to Cracow, where he recovered some of the Medici cash from the Poles but did not return it to the Medici. Eighteen years later, hearing that Tornaquinci had fallen into poverty in Poland, Giovanni di Bicci sent him 36 florins, enough to live on for a year and more. In the end, we know very little about Giovanni, but it's hard not to warm to someone who could show charity to an employee who had behaved so badly.

AS WELL AS choosing the right manager, one also had to get the right pope. When Giovanni di Bicci became Giovanni XXIII's banker, there were actually three popes in vitriolic and even bloody conflict with each other: Giovanni in Rome, Benedict in Avignon, Gregory in Naples. In the second story of the *Decameron,* Boccaccio suggested that it was precisely the perverse antics of the Church, its corruption and interminable internecine quarrels, that demonstrated the resilience of the Christian faith. People went on believing regardless. All the same, three popes presented a serious administrative headache. Who makes the clerical appointments? To whom do I pay tithes? Who will shrive me? Weary of the division, the Holy Roman Emperor invited all contenders to a Church Council in Constance in 1414 to settle the matter. Giovanni XXIII, who was at that point taking refuge from his various enemies in Florence, set off, and with him the Rome branch of the Medici bank. The Rome branch—take this as read from now on—always travels with the pope and his entourage. In the end, for banking purposes, Rome is the Curia, the papal court. What has there ever been in Rome, Italians still complain, but bureaucracy, ecclesiastical or secular?

Everywhere the pope went, food and accommodation prices rose, endearing him to some and half-starving others. And what with three popes and all the cardinals arriving from all over Christendom and moving a great deal of money back and forth, the Italian banks did good business in Constance. Cosimo, now twenty-five, having just married Ilarione's distant cousin, Contessina de' Bardi, joined his in-law to get some experience and meet some useful people. Alas, their pope came out the loser. After some tortuous diplomacy, Baldassarre/Giovanni, sensing things were not going his way, tried to scuttle the council, upon which he was arrested and accused of heresy, incest, piracy, simony, sodomy, tyranny, murder, and fornication . . . with more than two hundred women. Perhaps there is a wild leverage in matters of morality as well as in banking. You are the world's spiritual leader, or the worst of all villains. You are singing in paradise or utterly damned. In any event, the culprit ceased to be pope, and in fact, so far as the Church was concerned, never had been. Hence the title of Giovanni XXIII was still available for a less-ambiguous candidate five centuries later. Meantime, the Rome branch of the Medici bank split, one half staying with the now-imprisoned Baldassarre/Giovanni and the other attaching itself to the new Pope Martin V, the two other papal pretenders having wisely retired from the field.

THE TALE OF Giovanni XXIII's vicissitudes—his four-year imprisonment, the Medici's remarkable loyalty to him, his bequest to them of the sacred finger of John the Baptist, their payment of 3,500 florins to ransom him, his assignment to them of his collection of rare jewels, their successful intercession with Martin V (after returning to the Curia a certain fabulously bejeweled mitre) to have their friend named on his release, whores and heresies forgotten, bishop of Tusculum (Frascati)—all this would be story enough to fill a book. Yet often it is not the obvious melodrama that really changes things, nor even the bewildering back-and-forth of money and sacred objects, but something quite different, apparently innocent. What mattered most in this tale—for the Medici, their bank, for Florence, and arguably, as we shall see, for us too—was Baldassarre/Giovanni's funeral monument. For in 1419, six months after he was ransomed, the ex-pope coughed up, in Cosimo de' Medici's house, that final debt whose payment you can only put off for so long.

Let us return for a moment to the first story of the *Decameron*. Ser Ciappelletto, notorious liar, cheat, fornicator, murderer, and sodomist (the list begins to look familiar), a notary by profession, is sent to a foreign country to do some debt collecting. He lodges with the local Italians, who, true to the nation's international vocation, are usurers. He falls mortally ill. They are terrified: if their guest doesn't confess, he will be denied burial; if he does, the scandal of the company they are keeping will offer local people the excuse they are looking for to lynch them for their usury. But Ser Ciappelletto has a solution. He confesses himself, yet claims to remember no worse sins than having once spat in church and once cursed his mum when he was a little boy. No, he never lent money at an interest. No, he never had sex with anyone. He preserved his virginity. Convinced the man is a saint, the priest has him buried in the local convent, where his tomb becomes an object of frenetic popular devotion; those who pray over it claim miraculous results.

The comedy of the story depends on the absolute clarity of the underlying theology and metaphysics. This world is a trial for the next. Death is the day of reckoning, after which it is hell or heaven (purgatory being just a more or less extended annex of the latter). To tell lies, then, in a final confession is madness. It turns the world upside down. Ser Ciappelletto is quite brilliant in the way he resolves an earthly problem, but utterly blind because he does so at the expense of his soul. He is going to burn. Human astuteness, which is so seductive, so funny, has no place in a vision that divides the world into good or bad and sees no space between.

It is precisely this clarity, then, and people's complete conviction in it (atheism is unimaginable), that leads to all the equivocation when it comes to describing complicated financial activities. For everything must be declared a sin or not a sin. "He who is not for me is against me," Christ said. In the Baptistery, Florence's oldest, most central church, a *Last Judgment* divided the domed ceiling into the blessed and the damned. Nothing else. The rigid, static Byzantine style, the hard little stones of the mosaic, allowed for no confusion, or even diversion. The image *is* its message. The beauty of color, line, and gesture only increases the clarity. For me or against me. Your fate. What could a banker do?

We know nothing of Giovanni di Bicci's childhood. Presumably, like other middle-class youngsters, he was signed on at a guild in his teens and was working in his uncle's bank as an adolescent. But for his sons he chose a more sophisticated education, first at a monastery school, then under the supervision of Roberto de' Rossi, a humanist from a patrician family, a man who introduced the young Cosimo and his brother Lorenzo to other more celebrated early humanists, Poggio Bracciolini, Leonardo Bruni, Niccolò Niccoli, and Ambrogio Traversari—men who instilled in the young banker a passion for the pre-Christian, classical world, and above all for finding, collecting, and even reading the manuscripts through which that world could be known. So while Cosimo was at the Church Council in Constance, and hence skipping his regular discussion groups with these men, he could enjoy the company of Poggio Bracciolini, who was present as secretary to Giovanni's papal court and who took time out from his duties to visit the monasteries of Cluny and St. Gallen, where he uncovered various forgotten manuscripts of Cicero and Quintilian. About these much could be said, but for the essential, though rarely declared, inspiration that lies behind early humanism, we can go back a generation and read Boccaccio's preface to his compendium book, *De mulieribus claris,* "About Famous Women." "I have decided to exclude Christian women," Boccaccio begins apologetically. Of course they are "resplendent in the true and unfailing light," but, "their virginity, purity, holiness and invincible firmness in overcoming carnal desire" have already been amply praised "by pious men outstanding for their knowledge of sacred literature." So I am going to turn elsewhere, Boccaccio tells us, to the pre-Christian world.

Christianity is duly acknowledged and revered, so that then we

Tomb of Pope (or anti-pope) Giovanni XXIII, commissioned by Cosimo de' Medici from Donatello and Michelozzo, in the Florence Baptistery. Warned not to disturb the Byzantine austerity of the space, the architects built upward rather than outward, but lavishly. The sculpted words, IOHANNES XXIII QUONDAM PAPA *("John XXIII, erstwhile Pope"), offered disturbing food for thought for Florentine worshippers.*

can concentrate elsewhere—on the women of Rome, the literature of Greece, on human qualities and values that have nothing to do with religion. This, more than any particular content, is the sense of humanism: to carve out a space that need not be understood in the urgent and inconvenient tensions of Christian metaphysics—heaven or hell—while still remaining within the Christian world. Dogmatism is abandoned, but not the faith. Is it really okay, Boccaccio had asked his mentor Petrarch some years before that preface, for a Christian to spend so much time with profane literature? So long, Petrarch assures him, as the literature is instructive, educates the young to serve the community, and turns the soul toward beauty and truth. This is the breakthrough: the idea of a secular space where one can have such moral values, but *independently* of Church teaching. What would-be honest banker dealing in dry exchanges would not yearn for such a thing, would not contribute to a culture that recognized other qualities than strict adherence to canon law? It is the space we live in today. Much of it was first staked out in fifteenth-century Florence.

In the medium of writing, creating this territory must have seemed easy enough: one rediscovered the literature of Rome and later Greece, made new copies, discussed it, wrote books about it. But the visual arts were almost entirely devotional in nature. How would the secular ever find some elbow room here? Slowly, is the answer, by stealth. The Medici played their part.

Of the four illustrious men appointed as executors of Baldassarre/Giovanni XXIII's will, one was his banker, Giovanni di Bicci. The ex-pope wanted to be buried in the Baptistery, the oldest, the most holy place of worship right in the center of Florence. Only three other bishops had ever been buried there, and only in the simplest and sparest of stone boxes. Decoration on the walls was a rigid black-and-white marble patterning. Nothing must distract attention from the final division of the blessed and the damned on the ceiling.

Cosimo took over the venture and got together the young architect and sculptor Michelozzo and the versatile genius Donatello. The Merchants' Guild, which was responsible for the church's interior decoration, expressed scepticism. No fancy stuff, they warned. The tomb must not project into the floor space. The artists placed their work between two existing pillars that stood against the wall. It did not project, but rose, through a loophole in the rules, twenty-four magnificent feet up the side of the church. Above three marble bas-reliefs showing standing female figures—Faith, Hope, and Charity—rested the sarcophagus, on the side of which two naked angels unfurled a scroll. Above the sarcophagus, carved in marble, was a narrow bed complete with mattress and pillow; and lying on the bed, entirely human and apparently asleep, his handsome, intelligent face turned toward the congregation, lay Baldassarre/Giovanni, cast in gleaming bronze. Above the reclining figure, taking the monument even higher, rises the most elegant bedroom canopy, again carved in stone and with its curtains apparently just drawn apart, and at the apex of the canopy, a ring appears to fix the whole structure to a point where the wall of the church juts out. The scroll, held by the angels on the side of the sarcophagus, announced IOHANNES XXIII QUONDAM PAPA—"John XXIII, erstwhile Pope."

Was the monument obtrusive? It obeyed orders about depth. But the bronze did gleam so brightly in the early sunlight while morning mass was recited; the reclining figure was so very human, so clearly a man of character, and so evidently neither in heaven or hell, that it was hard not to be distracted. Above all, that inscription, "erstwhile Pope," brought a gust of schism and ambiguity into the eternally still air of the Byzantine mosaics. Had he been pope or not? Nothing is more inimical to the *diktat* of revealed truth than the complexity of human history. Martin V hated the monument. Baldassarre was never pope, he insisted. The Giovanni XXIII domain was still available. This man was the Medici's friend, people whispered. They paid for this tomb. How fascinating it all was! As if, in the niche of the medieval church, where one expected to find a rigid symbolic representation of this or that virtue, a real person appears, not easily judged or categorized. The effect is not unlike those moments in Dante's *Inferno* when one of the damned ceases merely to represent this or that sin and becomes a man or woman with a complex story, someone we are interested in, sympathetic toward.

Did the Medici banker know what he would be getting when he commissioned Baldassarre Cossa's tomb? We do not know. But whatever his intentions may have been—to honor a family friend, to embellish a church, to suggest the power of Medici money—Cosimo was a man who saw when there was a lesson to be learned. Something had shifted in the hitherto-timeless stasis of the church. From now on, Donatello would be Cosimo's favorite sculptor, Michelozzo his preferred architect.

3

The Rise to Power

Cosimo was thirty-one. It was 1420, and his father, turning sixty, retired from the bank. Piero di Cosimo, first of the next generation, was four. A second son, Giovanni, was on the way. The wife and mother, Contessina de' Bardi, was jolly, tubby, and practical. Uneducated, she was not allowed in Cosimo's study. Away on business, he rarely wrote. Marriages were arranged and that was that. She was a Bardi and he a Medici. Neither complained. On the contrary.

Taking over the bank, Cosimo went down to Rome for three years where Martin V's preferred bankers had just failed and the Medici were back in the papal saddle again. A relief. What kind of man is Cosimo? Polite, unostentatious. He prefers a mule to a horse. Challenged, he is pithy and cryptic. "Cosimo, I wish you would say things clearly so I could understand you." "First learn my language," he replies. "Cosimo, how should I behave on this diplomatic mission?" "Dress like a lord and say as little as possible." It's a style that allows you to be smart, without giving much away. To confide in a man is to become his slave.

Cosimo loves collecting books, religious and profane. Reading one entitled *Monastic Institutes,* he marks passages stressing patience and discretion, and what to do about the temptations of the flesh. In Cicero's *On Oratory,* he notes that an audience may often be won over if you *appear* to take the majority opinion. Interesting reflection. He's not interested in jousting or piazza sports. But he is a member of a religious confraternity. People get together once a week to sing praises to God, give each other a penitential whipping, and plan street processions in honor of patron saints. Cosimo commissions a fancy bas-relief chest from Ghiberti to hold the relics of three obscure martyrs. He's fascinated by astrology and magic, but he loves banking. "Even if money could be made by waving a wand," he says, "I would still be a banker." Why? Banking involves manipulation, risk, power. It's magic that works.

Cosimo is immensely ambitious. The Medici family was once second to none. He is also immensely cautious. The Medici family was disgraced. In 1421, his father, Giovanni di Bicci, is elected *gonfaloniere della giustizia* (standard-bearer of justice), head of the Florentine government. It's the first time the honor (a two-month appointment) has gone to a Medici since Silvestro sided with the woolworkers' revolt in 1378. The family is on the up again, third richest in the city. Who knows what might be possible? But Cosimo is also constantly aware of his mortality. He was born a twin, his brother Damiano died at birth. And death means eternal judgment. What doth it profit a man if he gain the whole world and lose his soul? However many fine sculptures were made showing beautiful human figures, this ultimate truth could not be avoided. Cosimo's destiny was to steer a course between conflicting aspirations—power *and* security, earthly wealth *and* paradise. With patience. Discretion. Hiding ambitions behind majority opinion. "*Semper,*" was the motto he eventually came up with for himself, "always," together with the diamond as a symbol, something precious and extremely resistant. Nothing in the history books gives us a sense of the man's ever having been young. Unless perhaps during those three years down in Rome.

Thou shalt not gamble. This was one of the commandments a Medici employee signed up to when he went to serve the bank in some distant branch. Years later, when Archbishop Antonino asked Cosimo to support a drive to stop the clergy from gambling, the banker replied, "Maybe first we should stop 'em using loaded dice." It was a religious age in love with transgression. There is no contradiction. Article seven of the Medici employee's contract said, "Thou shalt not keep a woman in the house." Your Florentine wife didn't travel, of course, and local liaisons meant scandal.

In the Eternal City, Cosimo settled in Tivoli. Deprived of stout Contessina's domestic skills, he asked an agent in the bank's Venice branch to find him a slave. The keeping of slaves had been permitted since the late 1300s after the plague had left the working population seriously depleted. The epidemic struck down men and women, old and young alike, of course, but the slaves brought in to solve the shortage—from the Slavic countries, Greece, North Africa—were almost all young women. She is "a sound virgin, free from disease and aged about twenty-one," Cosimo's agent told him. Quite an advertisement. Himself a declared devotee of the Virgin, Cosimo called the girl Maddalena, after a more ambiguous Mary, and some time later she bore him a child, Carlo, with marked Circassian features. We do not know how much embarrassment this caused, but clearly being a manifest adulterer was not as much of a problem as being a manifest usurer. No question of restitution here. Cosimo brought up Carlo in his own household together with the legitimate sons, Piero and Giovanni, and later used his influence to get the boy into the Church and have him become bishop of Prato. This was standard practice. It was considered appropriate for the fruits of carnal sin to take vows of celibacy. Hadn't Saint Jerome rather paradoxically suggested that the only purpose of procreation was to produce virgins for God?

One of the men Cosimo was working with in the bank in Rome, Giovanni d'Amerigo Benci, had a child by a friend's slave before marrying a much younger woman who bore him eight children. Then, when she died, he had another child from his own slave, who once again had been given the name Maria. A deeply religious man and brilliant accountant, Benci was to be the chief architect of the Medici bank's success under Cosimo and eventually spent some of the considerable wealth he accumulated in the process to restore a convent of cloistered nuns (known as the *Murate,* the walled-in ones) before whose altar this prolific man wished to be buried. Meantime, we have no more news of Cosimo's Maddalena. In a tax return of 1457, the aging banker would declare possession of four slaves, but their names and genders are not mentioned. Only their collective market worth—120 florins.

FOREIGN VISITORS TO Italy in the fifteenth century frequently remarked on two peculiarities: Everybody had illegitimate children and everybody was extremely concerned with etiquette. Of visiting foreign courts, the Italians observed that, deserving or otherwise, the monarchs enjoyed the blind loyalty of their subjects, who nevertheless behaved in the most slovenly fashion. Courtiers snacked and played cards in a French king's presence. How boorish the Germans were! What horrible eating habits! My life is at your service, the Italians said, deferring to their betters. I live only to do your bidding. But treachery was endemic. They bowed and scraped and stabbed you in the back.

The historian Jakob Burckhardt related the high level of illegitimacy to the general breakdown of dynastic order in Italy. All that mattered was power. With cash you could buy papal recognition of an illegitimate child's legitimacy. Does that make sense? And it was perhaps in the absence of order and under the constant threat of anarchy that etiquette and obeisance became so important. They gave a form to life, however superficial. All the art of the period, literary and pictorial, all the imaginative constitutional compromise, the obsession with precise accounting, the interminable rules about what could be worn and what could not, the huge output of letters, chronicles, reflections, and memoirs, might be seen, in part, as a reaction to encroaching chaos. Frescoed, the crowd or the battle scene became form, manageable, beautiful, less frightening. The court of Francesco Sforza, the bastard who, with Cosimo's financial help, would fight his way to being duke of Milan, gave the most punctilious attention to ceremony. Even before his wife became duchess, Francesco insisted that people call her *illustrissima*. She too was illegitimate.

But as well as this mime of decorum, there was also an Italian habit, still alive today, of seeking out, in the risky business that life always is, a protecting figure, not unlike a patron saint, who would intercede on your behalf with the powers that be—the taxman, for example, and the priest. It would not be long now before Cosimo the banker would become such a figure, the center of a network of families writing him letters of the variety, "Cosimo, you are our God on earth," or poems addressing him as "the singular refuge of all those/who live under the standard of poverty." Meanwhile, the Medici bank was expanding, Giovanni d'Amerigo Benci was sent to Geneva to do business at the city's big international fairs, and Florence, of course, was at war.

In fact, for at least the first half of this book—until the mid-1450s, that is—the reader can take it that Florence is *always* at war, and that these wars have fewer consequences for most people than almost any other war we are used to thinking of. To understand this strange phenomenon and how profoundly it altered the nature of the Medici bank and the destiny of its founding family—for no commercial organization lives in a vacuum—we must get a grip on the state of Italy in the early fifteenth century.

It's complicated. Because the country was fragmented into a score of small and even tiny states, historians like to say that the name *Italy* was "nothing more than a geographical expression." This is quite wrong. Italians were perfectly aware of a shared history, church, culture, and language (however varied its dialects). As a result, they were also aware that it might occur to someone to unite the country, as once it had been united under Rome. This is what they were afraid of. At the local level, they yearned for unity, the better to avoid it at the national level. Group identity and community pride were, and in Italy still are, very much a city thing.

Let us dispense with the "boot" image and imagine a cylinder topped by an inverted equilateral triangle. The cylinder is surrounded by the sea and mostly mountainous, the triangle is generally flat but shut off to the north by the Alps. There are five major players in the game. In the lower part of the cylinder, the Kingdom of Naples; in the middle, Rome and its Papal States; at the conjunction of cylinder and triangle, Florence; toward the top left of the triangle, Milan; at the top right, Venice. In between these larger states is a generous scattering of smaller ones, there to be gobbled up by predators, like fruit in a computer game.

All five larger powers are imperialist by vocation, if only because conquest tends to confer an aura of legitimacy on their leaders. You don't argue with a winner. Their overseas empire mostly lost to the rampant Turks, the Venetians are looking to expand inside the northern Italian plain (Verona, Brescia) and down the Adriatic coast (Ferrara, Forlì, Rimini). Conscious of the vastness of France to the north, Duke Filippo Visconti of Milan has his eyes on the western port of Genoa and various other towns to the south and east as a counterweight. The duke is rapacious, incorrigible, his emblem a snake swallowing a child. Despite its pacifist rhetoric and republican vocation, Florence has recently captured Arezzo, Pisa, and Cortona, and bought Leghorn (for 100,000 florins) to secure an outlet to the sea. Now the Florentines want Lucca, and perhaps one day Siena too.

In Rome, Pope Martin will be happy if he manages to gain some kind of real control over his small and turbulent client states on the eastern side of the cylinder, the Adriatic coast. Like any other duke or prince, he engages in military campaigns, his army commanders for the most part being bishops. No smiles, please. Just as a vow of celibacy doesn't stop a man from having children, so cassock and crucifix won't prevent him from being effective in battle. To the south, Naples is run by the Angevins, a French family whose members are also counts of Provence. Naturally, they are eager to expand northward from Naples and dream of eventually connecting up with their French possessions. Being about halfway between the two, the port of Genoa would seem to be the appropriate link, if only they could get their hands on it before Duke Visconti of Milan does. But meantime the Angevins' right to the Neapolitan crown is contested by the Spanish royal family of Aragon, which already rules Sicily. There are frequent skirmishes.

Given this play of forces, the pattern that endlessly repeats itself is as follows: One of the "big five" states—say, Milan—attacks a smaller independent town or towns. Inevitable military success arouses the suspicions of the other major players, two of whom—say, Florence and Venice—form an alliance. When Milan's next victim sends out an SOS, the allies dive in. They too seize a few towns but then get suspicious of each other. Milan strikes directly at Florence to draw off a siege elsewhere. The Venetians move west to grab Verona and Brescia. The pope charges up the Apennines to the east, hopeful of subduing a couple of rebel towns while everybody is too busy to notice. Not to be left out, the Neapolitans march north. To help or hinder? Nobody is sure. Everything is fluid. Everything is up for grabs.

Or is it? Clearly, Rome has a special status. Not just a despot,

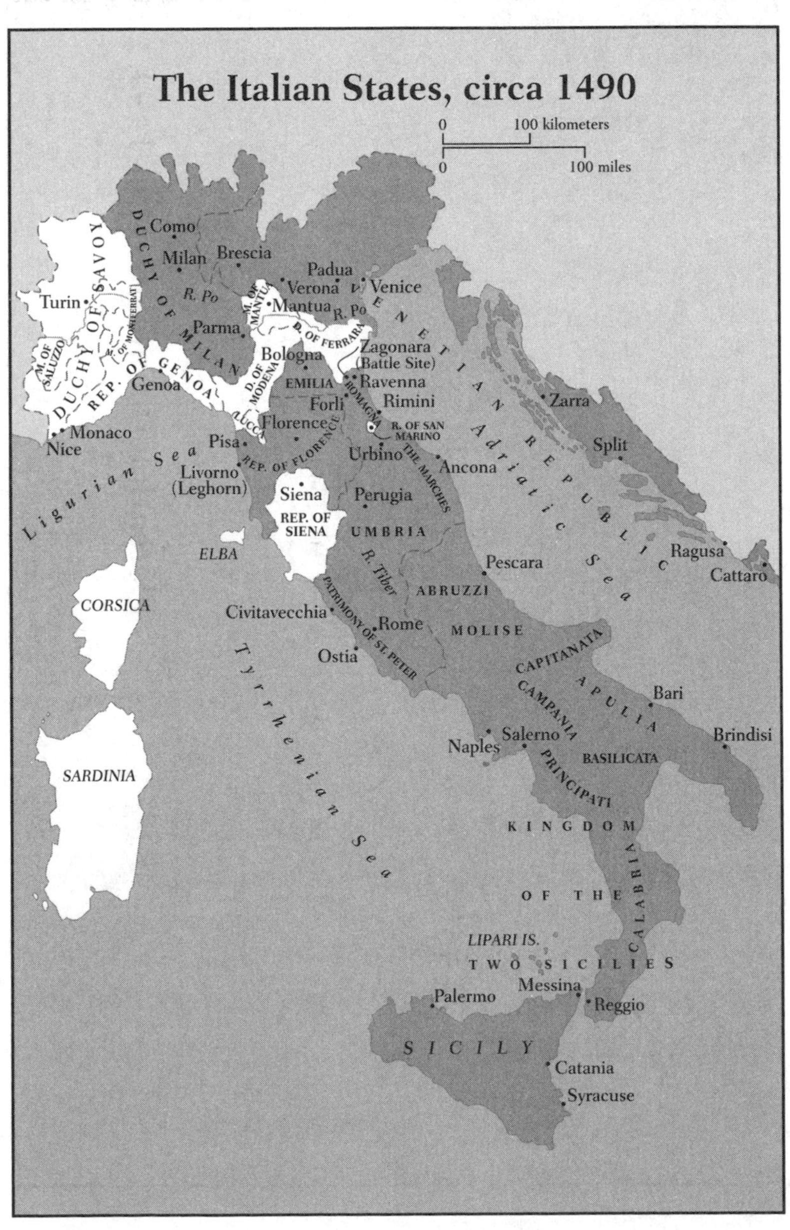
The Italian States, circa 1490
0
100 kilometers
0
100 miles
DUCHY OF SAVOY
DUCHY OF MILAN
Como
Milan
Brescia
Padua
Verona
Venice
Turin
R. Po
Mantua
M. OF MANTUA
R. Po
VENETIAN REPUBLIC
Parma
D. OF FERRARA
M. OF SALUZZO
Bologna
Zagonara
(Battle Site)
REP. OF GENOA
D. OF MODENA
Genoa
EMILIA
Ravenna
ROMAGNA
Rimini
Forlì
Zarra
Florence
LUCCA
R. OF SAN MARINO
Monaco
Nice
Pisa
Split
Urbino
Ancona
THE MARCHES
REP. OF FLORENCE
Adriatic Sea
Livorno
(Leghorn)
Ligurian Sea
Siena
REP. OF SIENA
Perugia
UMBRIA
ELBA
Ragusa
Cattaro
Pescara
R. Tiber
ABRUZZI
CORSICA
Civitavecchia
PATRIMONY OF ST. PETER
Rome
MOLISE
Ostia
Tyrrhenian Sea
CAPITANATA
APULIA
Bari
CAMPANIA
Naples
Salerno
Brindisi
SARDINIA
PRINCIPATI
BASILICATA
KINGDOM
OF THE
TWO SICILIES
CALABRIA
LIPARI IS.
Messina
Palermo
Reggio
SICILY
Catania
Syracuse

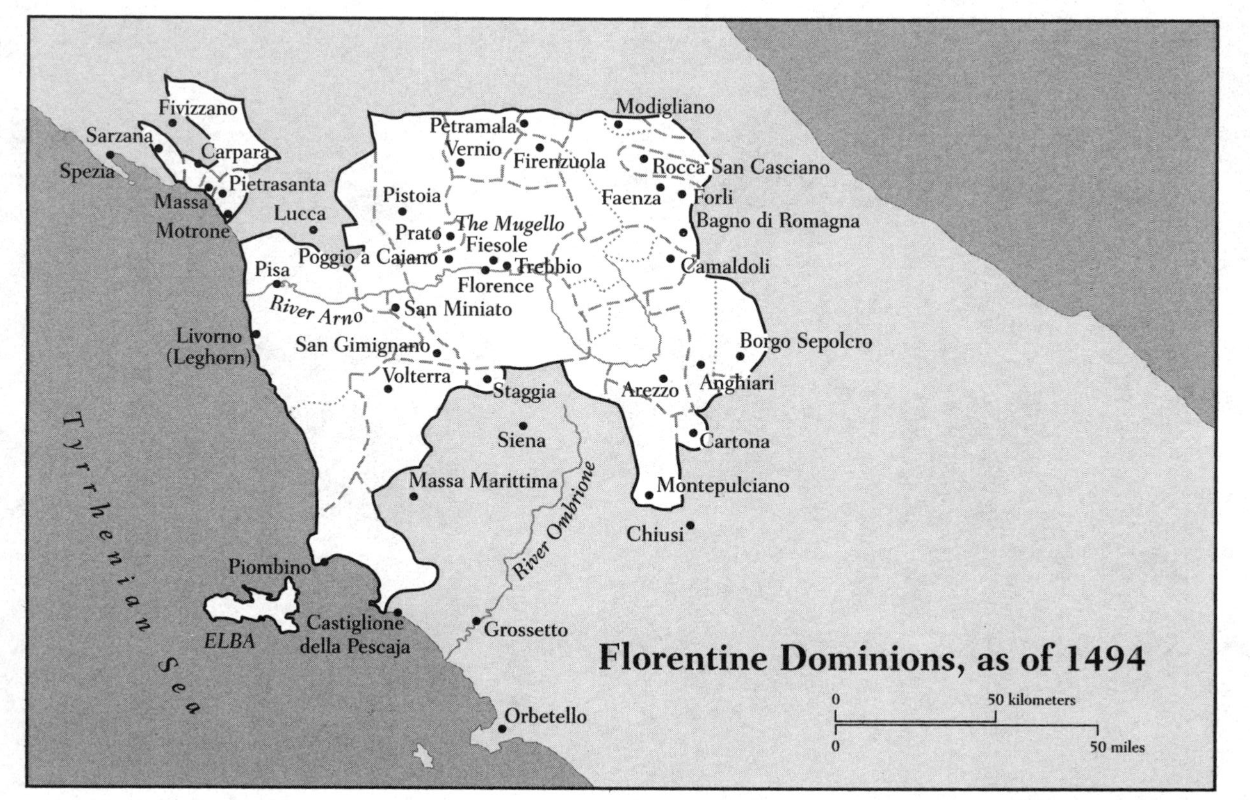
Florentine Dominions, as of 1494
0
50 kilometers
0
50 miles
Fivizzano
Sarzana
Carpara
Spezia
Pietrasanta
Massa
Motrone
Lucca
Pisa
Poggio a Caiano
River Arno
Livorno
(Leghorn)
Petramala
Vernio
Firenzuola
Pistoia
Prato
The Mugello
Fiesole
Trebbio
Florence
San Miniato
San Gimignano
Volterra
Staggia
Siena
Massa Marittima
River Ombrione
Modigliano
Rocca San Casciano
Faenza
Forli
Bagno di Romagna
Camaldoli
Borgo Sepolcro
Anghiari
Arezzo
Cartona
Montepulciano
Chiusi
Piombino
ELBA
Castiglione
della Pescaja
Grossetto
Orbetello
Tyrrhenian Sea

but God's vicar on earth, the pope, if seriously threatened, can order an interdiction, as he did in Florence in the fourteenth century. Then the priests won't perform your marriage ceremony or give you last rites or bury your dead. Without ritual, the world comes to a standstill. Rome, aside from moments of Angevin delirium, or internal republican revolt, is untouchable.

Nor, aside from brief interludes of Visconti aberration, do Milan, Venice, and Florence really believe they could conquer and absorb one of the others, since that would provoke an unstoppable alliance against them. Begun with great energy and straightforward goals, these wars immediately complicate. The combatants suffer a loss of faith. Armies get bogged down and confused. Winter comes. People are tired and cold. Eventually, they make peace and the prewar situation is reestablished, give or take a citadel or two. Even where a large city is captured, it is rarely integrated into the conquerors' territory. The Pisans, for example, conquered in 1406, do not enjoy the benefits of Florentine citizenship. Pisa is a subject town, a cow to milk, an outlet to the sea. Hence the Pisans are determined to rebel the moment circumstances are favorable. Gobbled up, the fruit is never properly swallowed. The game can start again, and always does.

Looking back on it all from the vantage point of the 1520s, Machiavelli was disgusted: "One cannot affirm it to be peace where principalities frequently attack one another with arms; yet they cannot be called wars in which men are not killed, cities are not sacked, principalities are not destroyed, for these wars came to such weakness that they were begun without fear, carried on without danger, and ended without loss." Without much loss of life and territory, that is. But not without the loss of huge sums of money. This is where the Medici came in. Even when it most resembles a sport, even when it is most futile, war is always cruelly expensive. And where war is never conclusive, a constant supply of money becomes absolutely essential.

BUT HOW WAS it that so few people were killed? Machiavelli puts it down to the tendency of the states involved to use mercenary troops led by professional *condottieri*. By-product of a decadent feudalism, the *condottiere* is a warlord with a private army. Many *signori* of small towns and citadels find that renting out themselves and their soldiers is the only way to stay solvent and independent. A *condottiere* without a small town has no scruples about acquiring one. An army needs a base. For the big players who hire the mercenaries, there is the advantage that few of their own citizens need risk death when war is declared. People can get on with business as usual. Also, there is no danger that some parvenu commander from their own ranks will attempt a coup. The last thing a state with a fragile government needs is some homebred, charismatic military leader.

The Italians were more advanced in the art of warfare than the other states of Europe and as a result their *condottieri* were much in demand in other countries. These men deposited their earnings with their preferred Italian bank—in Bruges or Geneva—and had the money sent home. However, since the mercenary soldier had nothing to gain from putting himself out of work, there was the drawback that the *condottieri,* particularly in Italy where they all knew each other, were notoriously disinclined to finish a job. "Enemies were despoiled, but then neither detained nor killed," complains Machiavelli, "so that the conquered only put off attacking the conqueror again until such time as whoever was leading them could refurbish them with arms and horses." Which meant spending a great deal of money, of course. Not to mention the fact that even when they lost, mercenary troops still demanded their wages. When they won, on the other hand, they had a habit of taking all the booty for themselves. In fact, in a certain sense, when you used *condottieri,* even when you won, you lost. In 1427, having spent the vast sum of 3 million florins in five years of war, Florence was plunged into an economic crisis that wonderfully clarified the political situation in the town. There was a dominant faction, headed by the Albizzi family, desperate to raise new taxes, and there was the immensely wealthy Medici family who, without actually proposing anything, had become a nucleus for discontent.

A state's ability to wage war is largely determined by its people's willingness to pay their taxes. That is a truism. "What was this wealth for?" Sultan Mehmet II would inquire of Constantinople's first minister after the great city finally fell in 1453. House after ransacked house yielded treasures withheld from the taxman. "What good are they now?" The first minister hung his head. "No price is too high for our liberty," Cosimo de' Medici liked to say; and he may have meant it, but when a wealth tax was imposed, he gave orders to the bank's directors to create fake accounts to limit the damage. "Most of the time tax returns are of no use at all for statistical purposes," regrets the historian Raymond de Roover.

Shortly after a disastrous Florentine defeat at the hands of

Milanese forces at Zagonara in 1424, an extraordinary sequence of frescoes began to appear on the walls of a chapel in the Church of Santa Maria del Carmine on the south side of the Arno River. Masaccio's *The Tribute Money* shows Jesus and his disciples being challenged by the tax collector as they enter a town beside a lake. Jesus makes a commanding gesture. In response, the fisherman, Peter, is shown at the left of the picture extracting a gold coin from the mouth of a fish that has generously given itself up at the water's edge; over to the right, the same disciple is already paying the coin to the taxman. Even Christ pays his taxes, the picture says. Even the Church. Pay up, everybody! On another wall the early Christians are shown sharing out their wealth among themselves in community spirit. But someone is lying face down in the dirt. Ananias didn't tell the truth about the price he got when he sold his property to pool the money with that of his fellow believers. He held a little back for himself. God struck him dead. The rich silk merchant Felice Brancacci, who commissioned this most beautiful of chapels, was himself a major tax evader. Like Cosimo, he held back a great deal. But then not all of us find gold coins in the mouths of fish. Being struck dead from on high is also rare.

I can imagine no better introduction to Italy and Italian politics than Machiavelli's *Florentine Histories,* inaccurate and biased as much of the book may be. It is the mindset that counts. To read a few pages describing how tortuous maneuverings were cloaked in noble rhetoric is to be amused. The idea of the spin doctor is not new, it seems. Of every diplomatic policy, the fifteenth-century Italian considered its *utile,* the hard results, and its *riputazione,* how it might be presented in the best light. "Then the Pope"—or the doge or the duke of Milan, says Machiavelli—"filled all Italy

Massacio's The Tribute Money, *in Santa Maria del Carmine (the Brancacci chapel). In response to Jesus' command, Peter, on the far left, recovers a coin from the mouth of a fish and, on the far right, hands it over to the taxman at the city gates. Tax evasion was endemic in fifteenth-century Florence.*

with letters," to explain why he had changed sides, perhaps, or why he couldn't help an ally in difficulty, or that he was fighting on behalf of liberty. It's a common refrain in *Florentine Histories*. Whenever somebody "fills all Italy with letters," you can be sure they are lying.

But to read perhaps thirty or forty pages is to get a little bored. Isn't there rather a lot of the same thing, of wars and betrayals and conspiracies? Even Machiavelli is weary. "While these things were toiling on in Lombardy," he doggedly starts a new paragraph. "While this war was dragging on to no avail in the Marches. . . ." Do I need to keep reading, you wonder? Yes. For at some point or other of the 360 pages you will be overwhelmed by a sense of vertigo, a delirium of treachery, deceit, wasted ingenuity, and inexhaustible avarice. This is the book's revelation. Absolutely nothing is stable. People seem to be taking a certain pleasure in betrayal and complex trickery, almost as if such vices were a novelty. Yet for all the twists and turns of combat and conspiracy, at a deeper level nothing really seems to change. Naples, Rome, Florence, Venice, and Milan remain independent from the beginning to the end of the century. As far as the smaller states are concerned, each new military campaign is just another shake of the kaleidoscope. It's difficult to fix any one pattern on the mind. Here below, tortuous as they will seem, are the events from 1420 to 1434 that catapulted Cosimo de' Medici from successful banker to political exile, then indispensable leader.

WHILE PRETTY SLAVE Maddalena treats Cosimo to Circassian pleasures in Rome, and Giovanni Benci opens the first Medici branch north of the Alps in Geneva, Filippo Visconti, duke of Milan, attacks Genoa. To avoid intervention from Florence, the Milanese duke has made a preemptive peace treaty establishing two spheres of influence: Lombardy and Genoa for Milan, Tuscany for Florence. The duke captures Brescia to the northeast and Genoa to the southwest. Fine. But all of a sudden he has an army down in Bologna as well, way over to the east, and now he's getting involved in a succession dispute in Forlì near the Adriatic coast. Fearing encirclement, the Florentines raise taxes and hire mercenaries. The treaty is dead.

One says the Florentines do this or that, but it must be understood that while the duke makes decisions rapidly and alone, the Florentines have all kinds of republican mechanisms in place that allow them to argue and procrastinate for days and weeks. The dominant Albizzi family is for war. Giovanni di Bicci is against it. Giovanni di Bicci has just been offered the honor of becoming count of Monteverde (a citadel to the south of Florence) by Pope Martin, no doubt in recognition of the very large loan that Martin somehow never gets around to paying back. Giovanni turns down the title. By Florentine law, a titled nobleman and his family are excluded from government. The Medici thus serve notice that they will not renounce their place in public affairs. Since the costs of any war fall mainly on the plebs—which in fifteenth-century Florence means the small-time artisans, woolworkers, shopkeepers, and so on—Giovanni's antiwar position is popular.

The duke of Milan (or his mercenaries) grabs the towns of Forlì and Imola to the east of Florence. The Florentines besiege Forlì. To draw off the siege, Milan attacks Zagonara. This small town is Florentine property, closer to home. The Florentines abandon Forlì and head for Zagonara. It's raining heavily. The men march for hours through thick mud and are routed on arrival. Thousands of horses are lost. "Nonetheless, in such a defeat, celebrated in all Italy, no one died except Ludovico degli Obizzi together with two of his men who fell from their horses and drowned in the mud." Or so says Machiavelli.

Not all *condottieri* are equal. As with sportsmen, there are regular players and there are stars. The Florentines get serious and hire Niccolò Piccinino. He's expensive. New taxes have to be raised. This time they begin to hit the rich as well. This wasn't part of the original plan. "It pained them," says Machiavelli of the wealthy families, "not to be able to carry on a war without loss to themselves." To make the tax unpopular and so have it withdrawn, certain subversive citizens insist that it be collected with the utmost severity. More people are killed during the tax collection than at Zagonara. Afraid that their grip on power is weakening, the Albizzi start to plan a coup that would restrict government to an inner circle of the most powerful families. But Giovanni di Bicci refuses to come on board, thus killing the project before it's off the ground and making himself even more popular among the plebs. Meanwhile, Milan captures all Florentine citadels and outposts in Romagna to the east of the city. The situation is getting desperate.

The expensive Piccinino and his men are sent on a mission to "persuade" the nearby lord of Faenza, ex-ally of Florence, to join them against Milan. Instead, Faenza fights the *condottiere* and, despite Piccinino's star status, defeats and captures him. Undismayed, Piccinino the prisoner manages to talk the lord of Faenza round. He will join the Florentine side after all. Rhetoric is an effective weapon. Once released, however, Piccinino himself changes sides and goes off to fight for Visconti, who has offered him more money. Money is even more effective. The winter break in hostilities, it should be said, often amounts to a sort of *condottiere* transfer market. Fees are rising. Some mercenaries hold discretionary accounts with the Medici bank. Or indeed other banks. What's the point of buying property with booty if someone else can then seize it from you? Money is more easily placed beyond the reach of enemies. The line between war and business is getting blurred.

"Bewildered by their frequent losses," as Machiavelli says, the Florentines now make the classic step of calling on the Venetians. The Venetians hesitate, unsure whether their preferred *condottiere,* Francesco Carmignuola, hasn't perhaps defected to Milan along with Piccinino. When Visconti tries to poison Carmignuola, it's clear that he has stayed loyal after all, and a deal can go through. Again the world is wishfully divided up: eventual gains in Lombardy will go to Venice, in Romagna and Tuscany to Florence. Having recovered from the attempted poisoning, Carmignuola is in venomous mood and captures Brescia, right in the center of the northern plain. A huge prize, for Venice. The Florentines are not overjoyed.

IT'S 1426 AND once again the coffers are empty, the city's debt is spiraling. Since the way of the world is that government is in the hands of florin people, it is *piccioli* people who end up paying most of the taxes. There are more of them. Paying a larger proportion of their wealth than the rich, they are discouraged from social climbing and the natural order of things is maintained. After an attempt to impose direct and proportional taxation a century before, in the idealistic days of the early republic, most taxation is now indirect. Carry a bucket of fish to town, you're taxed. Bring a cart of wheat to mill, you're taxed. The city walls are not just there to keep out enemies. As in Masaccio's, *The Tribute Money,* the tax collector waits at the gate. And don't try to hide that goose under your cloak, because he will check!

But it's not enough. Yes, there are plenty of *piccioli* people, but as we recall, it takes 80 or 90 *piccioli* to make a florin. And quite a few thousand florins to pay a mercenary army. During the thirteenth and fourteenth centuries, since the wealthy really did not want to give anything away, the government experimented with loans. The merchant, or banker, puts a handsome sum in the public coffers and collects a handsome interest rate (or gift) in return. Officially, it is just 5 percent, but as an incentive to lend to the state, you get 300 florins' worth of debt certificates for every 100 florins paid. So really you're earning 15 percent. The indirect taxes that the plebs are paying on salt and eggs and meat and wine and fats and oils are now funding the interest rates of the better folk who put down their lump sums years before. It's charming but it can't last. It doesn't add up. Mid-fourteenth century, the public debt has to be consolidated. The government announces that from now on, interest returns on tax loans will only be paid when and to the extent possible. As a result, disappointed lenders in need of ready cash start selling their debt bonds to those speculators who can wait. The Dominicans say this is usury and the

Franciscans say it is not. What do we have different religious orders for, if not for a second opinion?

In the early fifteenth century, the Florentine branch of the Medici bank became a major dealer in debt bonds, which by 1426 were trading at only 20 to 35 percent of face value. Clearly, the idea of the government's ever paying the interest was now considered a very long shot. The days of the willing lender were over. The government did try to raise money through forced rather than freely granted loans. The trick here was that if you agreed not to collect the interest, the amount you were asked for was drastically reduced. But in the end, these makeshifts just weren't enough. When people paid the full amount and wanted interest, the government couldn't pay. When they took the cheaper option, the income wasn't enough. And now there really is no more money to be squeezed out of the plebs. People are starving. The time has come to make the rich pay.

Two figures are presently manipulating the officially republican government: Rinaldo degli Albizzi, head of a rich landowning family, and the aging, highly respected Niccolò da Uzzano. Together they introduce the so-called *catasto,* or register. Every three years, every family in Florence will present a declaration listing all property, investments, and incomes. Certain deductions are allowed, certain complex calculations are made of the value of land worked by tenant farmers who pay rent in kind. For each declaration, a so-called *sovrabbondanza*—or excess of what is strictly necessary for staying alive—is established, and when the government needs money it taxes everybody 0.5 percent of that value. This wouldn't be too much if it were only collected once a year, but it could be demanded twice, or even three times a year. In 1427, 10,171 families make declarations and 2,924 are immediately exempted from any payment at all because *miserabili.*

The poor are thrilled. Taxation in proportion to ability to pay! At last. The big landowners complain that just because they hold property does not mean that they have the florins ready to pay the taxes on it. Many landowners do indeed find themselves having to sell land to pay what's asked of them. The merchants, on the other hand, are furious about having to declare liquid assets. Cash is here today, gone tomorrow, and easily hidden, they point out. All the law does is encourage evasion and the flight of capital—through the Medici bank, for example—while discouraging local investment. As soon as the law is enacted, almost all Florentine businessmen set about making false declarations. "For love of the taxman," a silk merchant's accountant writes ironically on the opening page of some rigged books. One Medici director invests sums in his own bank under three false names.

In the 1427 *catasto,* the first, Cosimo de' Medici declares possession of two factories turning raw wool into cloth. Opened in 1402 and 1408, these businesses employ a great many more people than the bank ever will but never make really significant profits. They serve to give the Medici a more solid and visible role in society. Florence, after all, is primarily a cloth town. The factories produce things people can see and hold in their hands and wear. They employ poor people. In 1433 a silk factory will be added.

The family also declares ownership of a villa at Careggi, just outside the town to the north, and a fortified villa at Trebbio, some miles farther north in the low hills of the Mugello, where the family also owns a great deal of agricultural land and again employs many poor people. A possible private army perhaps. In fact, it's time to stop thinking of the Medici, as just one family, or just a bank. Cosimo's older cousin, Averardo di Francesco de' Medici declares possession of Cafaggiolo, another fortified villa near Trebbio. The extended family controls important official appointments in the nearby towns of Scarperia, Borgo San Lorenzo, and Marradi. There are family chapels in the churches. Averardo also has a bank, albeit not as big as Cosimo's. The Rome branch is losing money, his 1427 declaration claims. A likely story.

Averardo is in partnership with a Bardi who runs things for him in Rome. On taking over the main Medici bank in 1420, Cosimo moved Ilarione de' Bardi up from Rome to Florence to be the bank's new general director and brought in a distant Bardi cousin, Bartolomeo, to manage things in Rome. These men are paid-up partners. Bartolomeo's brother, Ubertino, runs a bank in London that regularly serves as the Medici's English agent.

Then there is the Portinari family. Again in 1420, Cosimo fired the head of the Florence branch and replaced him with Folco d'Adovardo di Portinari, brother of Giovanni d'Adovardo Portinari, who is running the Venice branch. These two men are great-grandsons of the brother of Dante's Beatrice Portinari.

So now we have three powerful old Florentine families—the Medici, the Bardi, the Portinari—tightly knotted together in and through the bank. Or rather two banks. And actually it's four families, if we count Cosimo's brother Lorenzo's marriage to a Cavalcanti. Lorenzo himself is also a director of the bank. This is more than a financial institution. It's a political entity, a clan, a party even, in a city where to form a political party is treason. By law, there can be no declared divisions in this most divided of towns. No political campaigning. The government has recently banned the meetings of various religious confraternities. All that whipping and singing and praising God has often been used as a cover for political conspiracy.

Overjoyed to hear the wealthy whine, the plebs start to demand that the new tax system be applied *retroactively*. We've been paying too much for too long, they complain. For centuries, in fact. They look to Giovanni di Bicci for support. It would be a mistake to ask too much, he warns. Giovanni is good at playing wise peacemaker, at deferring the crisis, at having it both ways—the rich man with the poor on his side. Behind his bent old shoulders, Cosimo and Averardo are alert and ready.

Meanwhile, the papacy has at last brokered a peace treaty among Florence, Milan, and Venice. No sooner has he signed it than Duke Visconti goes on the warpath again, only to be soundly beaten by Carmignuola at Maclodio, near Brescia. Clearly, the turning point of this whole war was the failure to poison that *condottiere*. When peace is finally concluded in 1428, the Venetians get Brescia and Bergamo—a great leap westward for them—while Florence merely recovers the peanuts they had lost. There is no territorial acquisition to pay off a towering war debt.

Perhaps it was precisely this frustration that prompted the sheer madness of Florentine policy in the five years to come. In any event, departing this life in 1429, Giovanni di Bicci was choosing a good time to go, a rare moment of peace. Thirty family members (all male) followed the coffin, plus a long procession of officials and ambassadors, lenders and account holders. He was buried in San Lorenzo, a northerly stone's throw from the *duomo,* in a sacristy he had commissioned from the great Brunelleschi. Later, Cosimo had this most elegant of spaces decorated by Donatello. At the four corners of the chapel, he hung shields showing eight red balls on a field of gold, the Medici family's insignia, sign of things to come. From now on, San Lorenzo would be the Medici church.

"PEACE HAVING BEEN achieved outside, war began again inside," Machiavelli observes. As if this were some logical necessity. People were still fighting over the *catasto,* the wealth tax. Discrimination! the merchants raged. Our books are being checked by government inspectors who actually work for rival companies. As always, their strategy was to have the new tax so brutally and extensively enforced that its enemies would multiply. You'll have to register all the property in all the outlying territories too, they insisted. Some of it is owned by Florentines. You'll have to register every loom, every mill.

There were those in the government who felt that extending the tax was not a bad idea. The Florentines had a flair for bureaucracy, which is why we now have so many records of the city's history. So the process of bringing all the outlying towns into the tax register began. In protest, an eighteen-man delegation arrived from the small subject town of Volterra. We can't pay, they complain. They are arrested. On release, one of the men returns to Volterra and starts a rebellion. Niccolò Fortebraccio, a now out-of-work *condottiere,* is engaged to go and sort things out. Before he and his mercenaries arrive, the Volterrans have already rebelled against the rebels and the town is in Florentine hands again. But Fortebraccio doesn't want to be unemployed. In November 1429, he marches into the territory of Lucca northwest of Florence and, acting on his own initiative, captures a couple of small citadels. Suddenly, the Florentines are unanimous in deciding that the capture of Lucca is absolutely indispensable. Wealthy Lucca will be their compensation for the disasters of the previous seven years. As always when there is a war, the city forms a ten-man committee to decide military strategy, the so-called Ten of War. Now undisputed head of the Medici clan, Cosimo is on it.

A cloud of ambiguity hangs over these crucial years that bring Cosimo to power. But then a cloud hangs over everything to do with him: the bank, his patronage of the arts, his relationship with slaves, his foreign policy. When Rinaldo degli Albizzi proposed that the other patrician families get rid of him, the now-decrepit Uzzano is reported by Machiavelli to have pointed out how difficult this would be: "The deeds of Cosimo that make us suspect him are these: he helps everyone with his money, and not only private individuals, but the state, and not only Florentines, but the *condottieri;* he favors this or that citizen who has need of the magistrates; by the good will that he has in the generality of people he pulls this or that friend to higher ranks of honor."

Did Uzzano really say these words? Commissioned to write the *Florentine Histories* for a later Medici and a grand duke at that, Machiavelli admitted in a letter to a friend that he couldn't honestly say "by what means and tricks one [Cosimo] arrives at so great a height." Hence: "That which I don't want to say myself, as coming from me, I will make his [Cosimo's] adversaries say." And he makes Uzzano conclude: "So we will have to allege as the causes for driving him out that he is merciful, helpful, liberal, and loved by everyone." In a cash-starved town, Cosimo had for some years now been using his wealth to gather political consensus. To what end?

"It is hard for the rich to live in Florence, unless they rule the state." Such would be the comment of Lorenzo *il Magnifico,* Cosimo's grandson. And the implication was, if you don't control the state, the state will ruin you. You will become the object of punitive taxation deliberately aimed at confiscating your fortune. But was this just an excuse? Would it have been possible for the Medici to run a spectacularly profitable bank and to stay out of government? In Rome or Milan, perhaps it would. One can become only so powerful in the shadow of a despot. Insist on a loan repayment from a prince and he arrests you. A pope excommunicates you. Even in republican Venice, the doge was elected for life and that was that. You couldn't take his place, so you could hardly be feared either.

But Florence worked like this: To prevent anyone from ever becoming a tyrant, a new government of eight priors plus one *gonfaloniere della giustizia* was elected *every two months.* To prevent divisive election campaigns on party lines, the names of possible priors—men who met certain restrictive financial and family criteria—were written on tags and placed in a series of leather bags representing different quarters of the town and different guilds. Then nine names were selected *at random,* two priors for each of the four quarters of town, six from the seven richer guilds, two from the fourteen artisans' guilds, and one man, always from the richer guilds, to be *gonfaloniere della giustizia,* the head of government. That is, in order that no single man might rule, *everyone* must rule, or at least everyone in the wealthiest classes, but *briefly*. It was an idealistic solution but hardly practical when it came to deciding policies for the long term.

For two months, nine men who perhaps didn't agree with each other and were no doubt concerned about abandoning their businesses for so long were obliged to live together (waited on hand and foot) in the Palazzo della Signoria and run the town. They were not allowed to leave their posts. The ruler must be seen to be a public servant. This was the spirit of the constitution. But temporary and unprepared as these men inevitably were—who knew I was going to be elected prior until just a week ago?—the person whom they tended to serve was the leader of whichever family and faction was dominant.

Not completely, though. Not slavishly. It was delicate, this mechanism. Anything could tip the balance, especially now that some people had begun to sense the end of an era at hand, to see the Medici as an alternative to the Albizzi. So with each new *signoria,* some priors might be obeying one camp, some the other. True, the Albizzi family had been running the city very successfully for decades, but thanks to the debts run up in the war against Milan, things were now going seriously wrong. People were unhappy. A power struggle was in the cards. Perhaps the Medici could have kept out of it, but the vastness of their fortune attracted constant attention. Democracy depends on consensus,

consensus on persuasion. And what is more persuasive than money? A dramatically successful banker doesn't even have to open his mouth before people come running. If you give me a little more time to repay this loan, I'll support you when I'm on the *signoria*. If you give my son a job, I'll have a word with the priors about your tax problem. Perhaps this is what lies at the heart of our dislike of banking wealth. We are afraid we can be bought. We are sure others already have been, and that many can't wait to be. Despite all the taxation and forced loans, Medici wealth continues to grow. Perhaps growth for a bank means growth into politics. A clash between the Medici and the Albizzi seems inevitable. The war committee, with Cosimo sitting, appoints Rinaldo degli Albizzi as war commissioner—the political figure, that is, who follows the city's *condottiere* on his campaigns. The boss will be out of town. The Medici camp will take every opportunity to slander him in his absence.

Everything goes wrong. Plundering the countryside around Lucca to starve the town, the mercenaries behave with extreme cruelty. The citizens of Seravezza come to Florence to complain: Despite surrendering, we've seen our churches sacked, our daughters raped. Rinaldo, who hadn't been in Seravezza at the time, is accused. He is only involved in the war for his profit, someone says. This is Medici talk. Furious, Rinaldo abandons his post without orders. The architect Brunelleschi takes time out from building the dome over the *duomo* to try to flood out Lucca by diverting the river Serchio. The Lucchesi build a dike to block the water; then, one night, they break the ditch that the Florentines have built and flood out the plain where they are camped. Touché!

Inevitably, Lucca's despotic *signore*, Pagolo Guinigi, sends an SOS to Duke Visconti in Milan, who dispatches Count Francesco Sforza, star *condottiere* of all time. Alarmed, the Florentines buy him off. Sforza refuses actually to change sides and actually attack Lucca for Florence—That would be a blot on my honor, he says—but for 50,000 Venetian ducats (perhaps 55,000 florins) he agrees not to defend the town. How can you fight a war without bankers? To sweeten the pill of this treachery for the Lucchesi, Sforza gives them a hand to dump the tyrant Guinigi and turn republican. Now they're even more eager to defend themselves. Now the republican Florentines will have to drop their pathetic rhetoric about having started this war as a fight against tyranny. It's the city they want, the wealth.

Another appeal from Lucca to Visconti produces Niccolò Piccinino. Is there no end to Milan's resources? This time Florence can't afford to buy him off. This time Piccinino lives up to his star status by defeating the Florentines at the Serchio. Beaten, they take refuge in Pisa, just in time to stop a rebellion there. Which was lucky. Cosimo meanwhile has taken the very wise step of resigning from the war committee to "give others a chance to serve." Having rooted for the war like everyone else, the Medici have had the good luck of not actually being responsible for defeats in the field. People are blaming Rinaldo degli Albizzi. Meantime, the highly respected Uzzano has died, depriving the ruling faction of a certain gravitas. When an ignominious peace is made in 1433, the town is bitterly divided. "Every case that came before the magistrates," says Machiavelli, "even the least, was reduced to a contest between them [the Medici and the Albizzi]."

Is there any legal way to resolve that contest? No. If the real power in a state is unofficial, then any transfer of that power must also be unofficial. This is the modernity of Florence. As with many democracies today, the constitutional mechanism is only half, perhaps less than half of the story when it comes to appointing the executive. Profound shifts of power occur outside the legal framework. The problem for the Albizzi and the Medici is that the moment a real conflict is joined, the unconstitutionality of their positions will be evident. With what results, no one knows. Perhaps a return to constitutional legality, to a truly independent, randomly chosen government. Neither party wants that.

Time is on the Medici side. Cosimo is getting richer. The branches in Rome, Venice, and Geneva in particular are producing healthy profits, the first through collecting Church tributes, the other two through exchange deals along Europe's busiest trading routes. To the sick, cash-starved city of Florence, Medici money seems to possess curative powers. Cosimo has been draining the resources of the Florence branch of the bank to make extra loans for the war effort. If he held power, perhaps he would be even more generous. He would have the wherewithal to look after the city. People are beginning to make puns on the name Medici—doctors. And it's not just the surname. Cosimo's name saint, St. Cosma, and his brother, St. Damiano, were doctor saints who performed miracles of healing. Cosimo had had a twin brother, appropriately named Damiano, who died at birth. Now in his mid-forties, and ironically in pretty poor health, the leader of the Medici clan is well aware that Rinaldo degli Albizzi must see him as a threat.

On May 30, 1433, Cosimo transfers 15,000 florins from Florence to Venice, sells 10,000 florins' worth of personally held government bonds to the bank's Rome branch, and deposits 3,000 Venetian ducats in the Monastery of San Miniato al Monte and a further 5,877 ducats in the Monastery of San Marco. He and his father have given generously to the Church over the years. Now the sacred and the profane are getting very seriously mixed up. Hidden among the miracle-working bones of long-dead martyrs, or wrapped in what might have been Christ's shroud, Medici money is at hand to satisfy local customers if the political situation leads to a run on the bank—Cosimo mustn't lose people's confidence by asking them to wait for a withdrawal. On the other hand, it is safely out of the way should the Albizzi, or an Albizzi-controlled government, try to confiscate his wealth.

FOR MOST HISTORIANS, Cosimo is the innocent victim of what happens next. He is also a political genius. The unanimity of this paradoxical view is striking. Rinaldo degli Albizzi is written off as a tyrant and a prig. He was opposed to Cosimo's humanist friends, the historian Christopher Hibbert complains, because he saw them as dangerous for Christianity. A bigot. But Rinaldo was right. The humanists certainly represented the first step toward the secularization of the West. That is not to say they were not Christian. Had they opposed Christianity, they would have been swept aside immediately. But their interests lay elsewhere, and their determination to see each written text as the product of a particular period of history would ultimately lead to an entirely different view of the Bible. At the level of political institutions, as early as 1440 the humanist Lorenzo Valla would demonstrate, through able textual scholarship, that the supposedly fourth-century Donation of Constantine, by which Constantine the Great was believed to have granted Pope Sylvester spiritual and temporal dominion over Rome and most of Western Europe, was in fact a ninth-century fraud. The pope's rule was thus no more legitimate than that of any upstart *condottiere.* He too depended ultimately on money, military power, and false papers.

Cosimo supported the humanists and they him. Who else could fund them so generously? But who else funded the Church so generously? Pope Eugenius IV, who replaced Martin V in 1431, needed an efficient international bank. Cosimo advanced the cash for Martin's burial *and* the funds for Eugenius's coronation. Who wouldn't deal with such a man? Money has this excellent quality: It can hold the most heterogeneous elements together. We meet our enemies in the account books of our banks, who, more often than not, are funding both of the political parties between which we are supposed to choose when we vote. Lavishing finance on such a wide range of clients, Cosimo knew he was putting himself in contention with a ruling faction that depended exclusively on the support of Florence's old patrician families.

It's the summer of 1433 and the road to power is blocked. Whoever makes the first move will be most in the wrong, most exposed to a public backlash, but also most able to deliver the killer blow. Cosimo retires to his stronghold in Trebbio to the north of the city. He stays there until the fall. Far from being the genius politician, he doesn't seem to know how to proceed. Does he already consider himself indispensable? Is he waiting for the call to power, for an invitation to sort out the city's finances? He has already lent the city a staggering 155,000 florins, as a result of which the Florence branch of the bank has been operating at a loss. Finally the call does come. Cosimo de' Medici is requested to present himself at the Palazzo della Signoria, the seat of government. Three days after returning to Florence, on September 7, 1433, Cosimo walks the couple of hundred yards from his house to the big central piazza and enters the massive building with its tall, solid tower. Even today, the place radiates a grim authority. And at once he is arrested.

Under Florentine law, a man couldn't serve in government if he hadn't paid his taxes. At the end of August, the name Bernardo Guadagni had been drawn from the bag that supplied the *gonfaloniere della giustizia,* the head of government. The officials checked his tax situation. Until shortly before that draw, Bernardo had been in arrears. But then Rinaldo degli Albizzi had paid his taxes for him. What a coincidence that his name was drawn! Rinaldo now has the city in his hands and Cosimo is in a trap. This is what all the banker's money and genius have brought him to: a charge of treason, a sentence of exile or death.

THE GRAND TURNING points in the history of the Florentine Republic are marked by the summoning of a so-called parliament. At its most basic, the system of government is this: The eight priors and the *gonfaloniere* form the *signoria,* which initiates all legislation. In doing so, they consult two advisory bodies, the Twelve

Good Men and the Sixteen Standard Bearers, who, like the priors, are chosen by lot. The laws proposed are then ratified or rejected by the Council of the People and the Council of the Commune, each about two hundred strong, and again chosen by lot, but this time for four- rather than two-month periods.

The system can be unwieldy. Since there is a well-established difference of wealth and class between those whose names are in the bags for drawing the priors and those in the bags for the two big councils, it is not surprising that sometimes the councils repeatedly refuse to ratify laws that successive governments insist are vital. So when an impasse is reached, or when some particularly momentous and difficult decision must be made rapidly, a *parlamento* is called, which is to say a gathering, in the open square outside the Palazzo della Signoria, of all Florentine males over the age of fourteen. The principle is not unlike that of the modern referendum. Sovereignty passes directly to the people. But, notoriously, modern governments call referendums only when they are sure that they can bully people into voting as they should.

So, in Florence on September 9, 1433, as the deep, old bell of the Palazzo della Signoria booms out to call the citizens to their political duty, armed men are already circling the square and controlling each point of entry. Medici supporters are discouraged from attending. Cosimo can see a corner of the scene from his cell window. Dutifully—and this is always the way at these parliaments—the men who do attend vote for the formation of a so-called *balia*. The word *balia* just means "plenary powers." Basically, the proposal made at every parliament is that the people hand over their future to an ad hoc body of two hundred men chosen, of course, by the present *signoria,* thus bypassing the resistance of the Council of the People and the Council of the Commune. In 1433 the *signoria* meant Rinaldo degli Albizzi.

The *balia* has been called to decide the fate of the Palazzo della Signoria's illustrious prisoner. Rinaldo wants Cosimo dead. Rinaldo is a landowner, the Albizzi family is old and rich. But it is not a family practiced in the art of exchange. Rinaldo is neither a banker nor a merchant, and he cannot compete with his rival when it comes to transferable wealth, to loans and bribes and patronage. He knows that Cosimo is one of a new generation who will not be destroyed by exile, as rich men were in the past. He has understood that banks do not exist in space in the same way as a castle, a farm, or even a factory does. The man must be beheaded, he tells the *balia.* It's the only way.

But he can't swing it. Even the men he has chosen for the *balia* are divided. Cosimo has so many friends. So many citizens are indebted to him. They see a future in him. Unlike a similarly rich banker, Palla Strozzi, Cosimo seems willing to spend his money more widely, for the civic good, to get involved in public affairs. Given more power, perhaps he would spend even more, rather than shifting capital to other cities.

The charge against the accused is vague. Cosimo de' Medici has sought "to elevate himself above others." But don't we all? Put on the rack, two Medici supporters "confess" that Cosimo has been planning an armed rebellion with foreign help. No one believes it. It's not his style. Venice immediately sends three ambassadors to plead on Cosimo's behalf. The Medici bank has important business dealings with influential Venetians. The new pope, Eugenius IV, is also Venetian and from just the kind of rich merchant family that deals with people like the Medici. The Vatican representative is eloquent on Cosimo's behalf. The Church does not want its banker beheaded and Pope Eugenius has all kinds of sanctions at his disposal.

Then the marquis of Ferrara muscles in. He's another client who appreciates Cosimo's services. Lying as it does in the no-man's-land between Venice and the Papal States, Ferrara is an important ally for Florence. The members of the *balia* are impressed. The mobility of money, it seems, makes the fate of a banker an international affair. Had the Medici merely been wealthy landowners, they could have been dispatched without anyone's noticing. Paid by Cosimo's friends, Florence's only military leader of note, Niccolò da Tolentino, gathers his soldiers and marches toward Florence from Pisa on the coast. At the same time, Cosimo's younger brother, Lorenzo, is busy raising an army from among the peasants to the north of the city, where the family has its villas and agricultural land. Already the *balia* has been deadlocked for a week or more.

Back in his cell, under the roof of the Palazzo della Signoria, Cosimo finally agrees to start eating when his jailer offers to pretaste his meals for him. The man will be generously reimbursed. Visitors start to climb up to the banker's cell from the lower floors of the same *palazzo* where the *balia* is meeting. It's a sign that Albizzi is losing his grip. Cosimo is allowed pen and paper: Pay the bearer, he begins to write, this or that sum of money. And he signs. Bernardo Guadagni, head of the *signoria,* receives 1,000 florins, far more than his miserable tax arrears, paid by Rinaldo degli Albizzi, were worth. "He could have had ten times more," Cosimo later remarked, "if only he had known to ask." In return for his thousand florins, Guadagni fakes illness, stays at home, and delegates his authority to another prior, likewise bribed.

Suddenly, the moment to kill has passed. The Medici army in the Mugello is ready to march. Niccolò da Tolentino and his mercenaries are within striking distance. Under pressure from foreign diplomats, the banker Palla Strozzi, a constitutionalist who genuinely believes that wealth can and should keep out of politics, withdraws his support for the proposed death sentence. Needless to say, his money carries a lot of votes with him. Everything that happens, it seems, is the result of each participant's calculation of his private interest. There are no ideals involved. An ideal situation for a banker. On September 28, three weeks after Cosimo's arrest, fearing an attack from without and a rebellion within, Rinaldo at last backs down and proposes a sentence of exile rather than execution. Relieved, the *balia* gives him a majority. Cosimo is to go to Padua for ten years, his cousin Averardo to Naples, his brother Lorenzo to Venice. That should keep the family apart. Fearful that there may still be plans to assassinate him, Cosimo begs to be allowed to leave the city at night and in secret. Throughout the remaining thirty years of his life, he will never again allow himself to be so completely at the mercy of events.

WHAT DID COSIMO do in exile? Much the same as he had done at his villa in Trebbio before imprisonment. He runs his bank and waits. He behaves. The postal service is effective enough. After two months, a newly appointed *signoria* allows him to move to Venice, where he stays in San Giorgio Maggiore, the old monastery of his client the pope. Immediately, he offers to build the monks a new library and supply the books. The Venice branch of the bank has been making profits of 20 percent a year on a capital outlay of 8,000 florins. What better way to spend it than by making friends and building support? Cosimo has brought his own personal architect, Michelozzo, into exile with him, almost as if this kind of project formed part of a predetermined plan. When a distant Medici relative tries to involve him in a conspiracy to engineer his return to Florence with the help of Milanese troops, Cosimo scores moral points by reporting the scheme to the government of Venice, which passes on the information to Florence. This is hardly generous to the relative, but Cosimo knows that the Florentines are bankrupt, and that no one will lend the priors "so much as a pistachio nut." How furious they must be to think of Cosimo lavishing his money on libraries in Venice when he could be helping out in Florence. Every generous display of wealth abroad will turn minds at home. In 1433–34, the profits of the Venice bank almost double. Much of this is business lost to Florence.

And now the wars have begun again, the usual complicated mix of rebellion and opportunism. Pope Eugenius has fled an uprising in Rome and taken up residence in Florence. He needs his banker more than ever. He needs money to buy friends and pay mercenaries. The city of Bologna, part of the Papal States, likewise falls to rebels. The Venetians and Florentines form an alliance to put down the uprising. Milan wades in on the other side, and in the late summer of 1434, the Florentines are soundly defeated by the now-inevitable Piccinino near Imola. A disaster. Immediately afterward, to top it all, Rinaldo degli Albizzi commits the unpardonable error of allowing a pro-Medici group of priors to appear from the electoral bags. Why didn't he rig the election? Cosimo is invited back. Rinaldo's attempt at armed rebellion is headed off with pathetic ease by a few empty reassurances from Pope Eugenius. His only consolation a few days later when he himself is exiled will be a big told-you-so to the seventy other prominent men obliged to leave the city with him. Cosimo should have been killed: "Great men must either not be touched, or, if touched, eliminated."

Taking over the reins of power, Cosimo at once exiles the dithering Palla Strozzi along with Rinaldo, thus demonstrating that to have money and not commit it politically is folly. Why else do big organizations give to political parties? In short, the banker is back, he is revered, he wields unconstitutional powers, and he hasn't even broken the law. Such was and no doubt is the power of money. Historians choose to praise the bloodless nature of this transfer of power. "Yet it was tinged with blood in some part," Machiavelli reminds us. Together with four other citizens, Antonio Guadagni, son of Bernardo (the *gonfaloniere della giustizia* who had accepted Cosimo's bribe), left his designated place of exile to go to Venice. Given the city's good relations with Cosimo, this was unwise. The five were arrested, sent to Florence, and beheaded.

Donatello's David. *The first we know of this extraordinary statue with its effeminate boy hero is its appearance in the courtyard of Palazzo Medici. There were those who accused Cosimo de' Medici of approving of homosexuality.*

4

"The Secret Things of Our Town"

He was accused of being friendly to sodomites. The first we know of Donatello's *David* is in Cosimo's house. It is hard to think of a better advertisement for homosexuality than this life-size naked youth in polished bronze who slays a giant to place a dainty foot on the severed head and assume an erotic pose. *Hermaphroditus,* a book of poems dedicated to Cosimo, was publicly burned. It promoted sodomy, said celebrity preacher Bernardino di Siena. But Cosimo never used his power to abolish the Officers of the Night, the vice police who prowled the piazzas in search of serving girls with too many buttons, perverse men in platform shoes, gay lovers caught in the unnatural act.

He was accused of being friendly to Jews. In 1437, the Florentine government conceded explicit moneylending licenses to Jews, not to Christians. But there is no indication that Cosimo opposed the law obliging Jews to wear a yellow circle of cloth. A Jew was not part of Christendom and that was that.

He was accused of usury and tax evasion. You will go to hell for benefiting from his evil earnings, Rinaldo degli Albizzi had told the Medici sympathizers. After his return to Florence, Cosimo lifted restrictions on the so-called dry exchanges. It was one of the few transactions that all the theologians agreed was usury.

He was accused of hijacking church renovation for his own glorification, of kicking out other would-be patrons, of replacing the family chapels of enemies with those of friends, of trying to buy his way into heaven, of using excommunication as a weapon to recover personal debts, of being too friendly with priests who are "the scum of the earth."

He was accused of spending fabulous sums on a huge new *palazzo* while others starved, and of appropriating cash from the public purse to do it. "Who would not build magnificently being able to spend money which is not his?" his detractors complained. Blood was smeared on the massive doors of the new house. Designed by Michelozzo and situated on the via Largo, just a few hundred yards north of the *duomo,* the Palazzo Medici had, and still has, the forbidding look of the fortress about it. There were no windows at ground-floor level, just solid stone.

He was accused of cruelty and tyranny. He exiled so many and never failed to have the standard ten-year sentence extended before expiry. Families were split and letters censored. Up and down the peninsula, paid informers monitored the whereabouts of old enemies. Ingenious codes were developed to bemuse the city officials.

He was accused of using torture. Girolamo Machiavelli, along with two like minds, was "tormented for days before being exiled."

Palazzo Medici, the house that Cosimo built. Inside, there are two spacious courtyards; outside, the palazzo could be defended against all comers.

Re-arrested for failing to stay in his assigned place of exile, Girolamo died in prison "from illness or torture."

He was accused of directing Florentine foreign policy for his own personal gain. In 1450, he switched the city's support from the old ally Venice to the old enemy Milan, revolutionizing the system of alliances throughout Italy. Francesco Sforza, erstwhile *condottiere,* now duke of Milan, was one of the largest clients of the Medici bank.

He was accused of subverting and manipulating the democratic process, of rule by intimidation, of crushing all opposition to his authority, of running a narrow oligarchy, of shamefully elevating "base new men" who would always do his bidding. One Medici wool-factory foreman eventually became *gonfaloniere della giustizia,* head of the government.

He was accused above all—and this accusation contained and explained all the others—of *seeking to become a prince,* of attempting to transform Florence from a republic to a hereditary monarchy. Why else would a man build a house "by comparison with which the Roman Coliseum will appear to disadvantage"? Aging now, with the sagging cheeks and baggy eyes we see in all the paintings, Cosimo did not trouble to defend himself. He knew he was widely loved, by many adored. The popular poet Anselmo Calderoni addressed him thus:

Oh light of all earthly folk
Bright mirror of every merchant,
True friend to all good works,
Honour of famous Florentines,

Kind help to all in need,
Succour of orphans and widows,
Strong shield of Tuscan borders!

Marco Parenti, son-in-law of the exiled Palla Strozzi, was implacably opposed to Cosimo and determined to bring his exiled in-laws back. On the banker's death in 1464, however, he was obliged to remark on Cosimo's modesty in deciding against a state funeral. He also acknowledged his enemy's part in bringing peace and some prosperity to the city. People were grateful. "And nevertheless," writes Parenti, "on his death everyone rejoiced; such is the love of and desire for liberty."

Some time after the funeral, the government of the town chose to reward the dead Cosimo with the title of *Pater Patriae*, Father of His Country. Who is simultaneously loved and resented if not a father? However benevolently, the paternal figure holds us in check. Only the security he brings can reconcile us to waiting for his demise. Cosimo's achievement was to make his Florentine family wait thirty years, and then some.

TO HAVE A proper understanding of Cosimo's management of the Medici bank, one must study the 600 densely detailed pages of Raymond de Roover's *The Rise and Decline of the Medici Bank.* To gain a thorough grasp of the way Cosimo ran Florence while apparently retaining the role of an ordinary citizen, one must settle down for at least a week with the 450 pages and labyrinthine complications of Nicolai Rubenstein's *The Government of Florence Under the*

Medici. To have just some inkling of the ambiguity of Cosimo's relationships with the Christian faith and humanism, the contradictory impulses driving his commissions of so many buildings and works of art, one must tackle Dale Kent's exhaustive and quite exhausting *Cosimo de' Medici and the Florentine Renaissance*.

These books rarely communicate with each other. Sometimes you might be reading about three different, equally remarkable careers. Yet whichever side of Cosimo you are looking at, you are always aware of this fatherly man's special genius for *holding things in check*. What exactly? The destructive energies generated by the collision of irreconcilable forces: faction and community, Milan and Naples, commercial appetite and Christian morals, the love of liberty and the need for order. To hold the fort—the bank, the family, the state—in the midst of chaos, you must reconcile the irreconcilable. How? The language rebels. In the short term, is the answer, with the aid of considerable sums of money, a genius for ad hoc solutions, and the utmost discretion. Only a banker could have done it. When the money runs out, or is used without tact, your time is up.

In 1442, in his early fifties, Cosimo was the main supporter behind the formation of a new religious confraternity: the Good Men of San Martino. The idea was to help the "shamed" poor, those who had fallen on hard times but were too proud to ask for charity. The Good Men went around the town asking for donations, after which they brought relief and preserved anonymity. Fifty percent of monies collected were registered as coming from the Medici bank. The contribution is entered in the bank's books under the heading: God's Account.

The arrangement is emblematic of the way Cosimo works. A largesse with political implications is hidden behind a religious organization and the name of a commercial company. The amount of money felt to be coming from oneself is doubled by also having donations collected from others. The sense of guilt arising from sinful lending operations and constant tax evasion is attenuated. The danger of economic unrest in the town is reduced. By not asking for recognition or imposing yourself as benefactor, you actually attract even greater recognition. Most crucial of all to the scheme's success, however, was a genuine charitable impulse. "The poor man is never able to do good works," Cosimo wrote thoughtfully to his cousin Averardo. The poor get to heaven, wrote Archbishop Antonino, by bearing their tribulations with fortitude, the rich by giving generously to the poor. Such is the providence of social inequality. A Christmas or Easter handout of wine and meat distributed by the Good Men of San Martino cost Cosimo 500 florins, three bank managers' annual salaries.

BUT SUCH SUMS were nothing compared to the cost of that greatest irreconcilable of them all: How could an international merchant bank function when most European trade was going only one way—from the Mediterranean northward—a situation exacerbated by the fact that Rome was drawing huge sums toward itself in Church tributes without even giving anything in return? Had the pope, the Curia, been based in Paris or Bruges or London, how easy everything would have been! Italy could have sent silk and spices north, then used at least part of the income in situ to pay its dues to the Church. Not too much cash need have been moved. But the opposite was the case. The Italian bank had to recover not only the payment for products sent north but also the papal dues that it was responsible for collecting. This in a world where to move money in coin was extremely dangerous. Much of the territorial expansion of the Medici bank was undertaken to deal with this chronic imbalance. The upheavals that led to the bank's eventual collapse stemmed in large part from the growing desperation of the measures used.

In 1429 it was decided that the Rome branch would operate *without capital*. Deposits from clergy, together with what coin did arrive, would be sufficient. Other monies due to the Curia from abroad would provide the capital for other branches. This move freed up perhaps twenty or thirty thousand florins. Not a solution.

Inevitably, the debt of the bank's northern operations toward its Rome branch grew. They couldn't find ways to send the monies they owed. This was not too worrying when the operation in question was another Medici branch, but it was dangerous when the organization holding the money was an independent agent operating on the bank's behalf. In the first decade of the century, the Medici had established relations with such agents in London and Bruges. These were other Italian banks that collected papal dues and sold luxury merchandise for the Medici bank. They were under instructions to seek out quality wool to send back to Italy (and the Medici factories) in order to balance the flow and make the return trip worthwhile for the galleys that had brought Italian products north. The banks thus aimed to create the trade that they had come into being to assist and exploit.

But there was a problem. The English now wanted to work all their wool themselves and imposed severe export restrictions and exorbitant duties. The flow did not balance and never would. In 1427, Ubertino de' Bardi in London and Gualterotto de' Bardi in Bruges owed the Medici bank the huge sum of 22,000 florins, most of it due to the Rome branch. Those Bardi! Did their slowness in paying really have to do with problems finding merchandise or letters of credit going south? After all, holding someone else's cash interest-free is always convenient. Was there some connivance, perhaps, between Ubertino de' Bardi, a free agent in London, and his brother Bartolomeo de' Bardi, the Medici director in Rome? Not to mention the Medici's general manager, Ilarione di Lippaccio de' Bardi, in Florence. This couldn't go on. At some point, the Medici bank would have to form its own branches in both Bruges and London, if only to invest the income that couldn't easily find its way back to Italy.

ON RETURNING TO Florence from exile in 1434, Cosimo cut all the Bardi family out of his extensive operations. A clean sweep. What had they done in his absence? We don't know. The richest Bardi, related by marriage to Palla Strozzi and working for Cosimo's cousin Averardo's bank, was exiled. The man was dangerous. Averardo himself had died in exile. Bringing families together in complex relationships might make for strength, but it could also create the conditions for conspiracy and betrayal. Here was another balance that would have to be struck and restruck, year in and year out. What Cosimo's Bardi wife thought about it, we do not know.

The Portinari family now took the place of the Bardi. Running the Venice branch, Giovanni Portinari was one of the most important men in the organization. Still nervous about the political situation in Florence, Cosimo had shifted much of the home bank's capital to Venice. In 1431, Giovanni's brother, Folco, running the Florence branch, had died, leaving seven children. Cosimo took three boys into his own family: Pigello aged ten, Accerito aged four, and Tommaso aged three. All would eventually hold key positions in the Medici bank.

Was this what Cosimo, who only had two children of his own—two legitimate children—planned? That the Portinari boys, brought up in his home, would be more indebted to him, better servants of the bank than any Bardi could be? If so, it was an error. Nothing is less certain than the gratitude of those who have seen us in the role of father, those who have sensed, perhaps, that the real sons are being preferred. There was some question as to whether the Portinari boys had received all the money they should have when their real father died. Folco had had considerable investments in the Medici bank.

Meantime, it was another Portinari, Bernardo, son of Giovanni in Venice and older cousin of the boys in Cosimo's care, who set out for Bruges and London in 1436 to look into the ever-present problem of the trade balance. Traveling through the Alps on horseback, Giovanni goes first to the Medici branch that Giovanni Benci has set up in Geneva. With Paris in chaos thanks to the interminable Anglo-French War, Geneva is a big success. Merchants come to its four annual trade fairs from all over Western Europe; the town is thus an important sorting house for much of Europe's currency. Everybody needs credit; exchange deals abound. Merchandise from the north can be brought at least halfway to Italy, turned into cash, and then sent on by messenger. The city even coined a new currency for all international dealings at the fairs: the golden mark, first hint at the euro perhaps.

After Geneva, Bernardo rode on to Basle, where Cosimo had set up another branch—not to trade, but simply to service the cardinals and bishops meeting there in acrimonious general council since 1431. Papal authority was the matter in dispute. By 1436, the Church was once again on the brink of schism. Pope Eugenius, still living in Florence, had abandoned proceedings. The Holy Father's banker needed to have a sense of who would gain the upper hand, though of course he would never shrink from taking deposits from both sides.

Traveling on to Bruges and London, Bernardo's brief is to get the local agents to speed up their sale of goods sent by the bank and, even more important, the return of money to Italy. He has special powers of attorney to have particularly recalcitrant debtors taken to court and imprisoned. The sad truth is that your debtor priest in Basle is a safer bet than your merchant debtor in London. Threatened with excommunication through Cosimo's papal connections, a bishop must pay up. His livelihood and identity are at stake. But there were merchants who took no more notice of a bull of excommunication than a *condottiere* would of this or that count's title to some citadel or town. "If only he was a priest," comments one Medici accountant, preparing to write off a bad debt, "there might be some chance."

But the real reason for Bernardo Portinari's trip north was to see if conditions were favorable for opening Medici branches in Bruges and London. Were the local merchants solvent? Were the judges fair to foreigners? What was the level of anti-Italian sentiment in the English wool trade? Considerable. Would the king waive the wool-export monopoly run by the English Merchants of the Staple if the Medici bank lent him ready cash? If lent cash, would the king pay it back? Was the Anglo-French War threatening trade between London and Bruges? How long was the king likely to be king anyway?

Bernardo Portinari's father died while he was away. He returned to Italy, gave a positive report, then went back to England with a papal bull regarding the appointment of the bishop of Ely and the collection of 2,347 Flanders *grossi* (about 9,000 florins), much of which was dispatched to Geneva hidden in a bale of cloth. Risky stuff. But profitable. In 1439, a Bruges branch was opened with a secondary office in London. The initial capital was a mere 6,000 florins, all provided by the branch in Rome. In 1446, London became a branch in its own right, with capital of £2,500. At this point, the Medici bank has eight branches of its own and agents in at least eleven other banking centers.

FROM THE GREEN-CLOTH–COVERED table in via Porta Rossa, from the palatial rooms of his great house, now home to the Medici holding, from his private prayer cell in the Monastery of San Marco, Cosimo's mind reaches out across Europe. He has no phone, no e-mail. The letters arrive regularly, bringing last week's exchange rates, coded secrets, the latest politics and war news.

Replies are dictated, copies made. The director in Rome is complaining about the director in London. I won't accept second-rate cloth as payment! I want cash. The duke of Burgundy is again defying the French. The coin arriving from Geneva is no longer current and will have to be re-minted. Aren't my managers spending too much time retrieving money from each other? That boy you sent us, Bruges objects, he can't even read or write! Why won't the women of Flanders buy Florentine silks? Our sales rep is so handsome, speaks French so well! You were told not to underwrite insurance on shipping, Cosimo reminds London. The ship was sunk *before* the premium was paid! Perhaps the theologians are right in complaining how exchange deals in Geneva always run from one fair to the next. It amounts to a loan with interest. But what can a banker do? What can I do to pay less tax? The balance sheet must show only half of the capital invested, Cosimo instructs the director of the Venice branch. And then there was Lubeck. Will the Hanseatic League never let us into Eastern Europe?

Cosimo has Giovanni Benci beside him now as general director of the Medici holding. They work together among the tapestries and sculptures of Cosimo's house. Benci had made quite extraordinary profits in Geneva. He is astute and gifted and devout. Pondering the accounts together by the light of an open window, do the two men occasionally exchange a snigger over the slave girls, the days in Rome? Are they in agreement with the general Florentine complaint that it's getting hard to distinguish an honest girl from a prostitute? Do they discuss their contributions to religious institutions, exchange the names of favorite artists—

Donatello, Lippi—discuss the latest translations of Cicero, the seductive ideas of the humanists? Why aren't the Florentine whores happy to wear bells on their heads? Why can't the Western and Eastern churches agree about the nature of the Trinity? Does the preacher Bernardino di Siena really believe, as he has been claiming in his sermons, that Jews take delight in pissing in consecrated communion cups? Cosimo is now an important figure in the religious confraternity dedicated to the Magi. Contessina fusses over what cloaks he should wear when he rides down the city streets to reenact the three kings' adoration of the Holy Child.

Together, Giovanni Benci and Cosimo open a Medici branch in Ancona in 1436. This Adriatic port was important for exporting cloth to the East and importing grain from Puglia, farther down the coast. But could that justify the huge capital investment of around 13,000 florins, far larger than the Medici investment in the more important commercial centers of Venice and Bruges? Florence was at war. Once again the Italian scenario was fantastically complicated: a succession dispute down in Naples between the Angevin and Aragon families; the two *condottieri,* Francesco Sforza and Niccolò Piccinino, at each other's throats in the Papal States; the pope marooned in Florence, afraid of going back to Rome, worried about developments in Basle, casting about for allies; Duke Filippo Visconti in Milan, with Piccinino in his pay, seeking to capitalize on the turmoil in every area, sending expeditions to Genoa, Bologna, Naples. And now Rinaldo degli Albizzi has left his place of exile and is begging Visconti to attack Florence and restore his family's faction to power. Undaunted, the incorrigible Florentines are once again launching an assault on Lucca and calling on the Venetians to help them out when it comes to the crunch with Milan. We would, if the Mantuans hadn't switched sides, the Venetians reply. In the midst of this confusion, Cosimo made a long-term decision to back the great soldier Sforza. The money down in Ancona was not to finance trade at all. Or not exclusively. Ancona was in Sforza's sphere of operation. It was the Medici bank's first serious move into funding military operations that were not specifically to do with Florence. Why?

In Milan, the fat, mad, aging Visconti had no legitimate offspring, just one bastard daughter, Bianca. Sforza wanted her for his wife, together with the Milanese dukedom. He wouldn't fight *against* Visconti while that marriage was in the cards. Or not north of the Po, in Visconti's sphere of influence (he later changed his mind). At the same time, the combination Sforza–Visconti, should the *condottiere* fight *with* the duke, was the one feasible alliance capable of inflicting decisive military defeat on Florence. The duke had tied Sforza's hands with the tease of his daughter, constantly promising that the marriage was about to take place, then inventing reasons for delay. Cosimo responded by tying the *condottiere* with his cash. Sforza could hardly fight for Visconti and the Albizzi if his army was fed and clothed by the Medici.

The Ancona adventure, though short-lived, marked a turning point in the history of the bank. It fused its destiny with that of the Florentine state. Here was a branch that lent mainly for political purposes, without expecting to recover its capital. Not good news for the small investor. Matters of state go beyond the rationale of any commercial venture. Thirty years later, Sforza would owe the Medici bank something in the region of 190,000 florins, a sum far beyond repayment. This was how the Bardi and Peruzzi banks had gone under years ago. But in 1440, Piccinino, Milan, and the Albizzi faction were decisively beaten by the Florentines at Anghiari, just to the north of the city. Sforza, the most successful military adventurer of the fifteenth century, was up north fighting in the Veneto. He never attacked Florence, despite the fact that the Florentines were his future father-in-law's bitterest enemies.

IT WAS THE period of the bank's maximum expansion. In 1442, a branch was set up in the subject coastal town of Pisa, whence the Florentine galleys set out every spring for Bruges and London. State-built and with a monopoly on all sea trade in and out of Pisa and Florence, the galleys were rented to merchants who then sold space to others. The right to rent for each voyage was auctioned off in a contest that lasted an hour, or the time it took for a particular candle to burn out. The smarter merchants waited till the flame began to gutter before beginning to bid. So it was decided that the auction would end with the chiming of the clock on the tower of the Palazzo della Signoria—audible but not visible from the auction room. Without a wristwatch, this was nerve-wracking stuff. The *palazzo*'s clock-minder was put under armed guard for the duration, lest the hour should shrink or expand. In this etiquette-obsessed world, cheating is the rule. Alertness is all. Nobody is fooled, for example, when the auctioneer plants dummy bids to get things going.

To set up a branch of the bank meant finding a house with a suitable room for the obligatory green table, as well as storage space for goods in transit. The half-dozen employees would then live and eat there together. To oversee the new venture in Pisa, Cosimo went to the town himself. For a two-month stay away from home, he took with him a trunk of books and his best ceremonial armor. He collected the stuff: swords with red velvet sheaths, painted lances, a silver-decorated helmet with a crest in the form of a gilded eagle, a shield picturing a young girl. He also collected books, of course, and was friends with Florence's leading humanists, who wrote or translated those books and often dedicated them to him. Common to the two areas of interest—books, arms—was the vision of a noble, superior man with an innate dignity that had nothing to do with Christian humility, the kind of dignity that painters and sculptors were learning to conjure up in the faces and postures of their figures.

"Only the little people and lower orders of a city are controlled by your laws . . . ," says a speaker in one of humanist Poggio Bracciolini's philosophical dialogues. Cosimo had once taken time out with Poggio to explore Roman ruins in Ostia. "The more powerful civic leaders transgress their power." That was an interesting idea, for a civic leader. It referred to the kind of man, surely, who, if he hadn't suffered from crippling gout, might have worn a helmet with a gilded eagle.

Along with all the calculation of profit and loss, there is, then, in Cosimo's mind, an ideal of fame and fine deeds that will survive the grave. "All famous and memorable deeds spring from injustice and unlawful violence," says Poggio's man in the dialogue. What a shame, Cosimo complained, that they had never captured Lucca! Perhaps one day, if sufficiently well paid, Francesco Sforza would help them do that. Then he, Cosimo, would be remembered as the city's leading citizen when Lucca was taken, as the Albizzi family, though exiled, was still remembered for having taken this proud town of Pisa, where, as always when establishing a new branch, Cosimo now faced the problem of how to register the operation. If a branch was registered with the Medici name, it would have more prestige and attract more investment. But in that case, the Medici holding would have to assume unlimited liability. If it took the name of the resident local partner who actually ran the branch, then Medici liability was limited to the capital actually invested, but the branch's prestige would suffer. Despite his ceremonial armor and incendiary reading, cautious Cosimo almost always opted for the latter solution, at least for the first few years. The Pisa branch opened under the names of Ugolino Martelli and Matteo Masi. In 1450, when serious losses forced the Medici holding to put a limit on its liability in the London and Bruges branches, which thus renounced the Medici name and emblem, the other Italian merchants took pleasure in the reversal and "cawed like so many crows." Like profit and loss, renown and ridicule are never far apart.

One wished to be honored long after one was dead, like a Roman senator (Cosimo collected Roman coins as well), but by that time, surely, the superior man would have humbled himself before his Maker and flown to heavenly glory, where such earthly honor could hardly matter. There was even the danger that chasing earthly honor might cost you your place in heaven.

Here, then, was another set of irreconcilables, and if the conundrum this time lay in the mind, or in metaphysics, rather than in the balance of world trade, it was no less urgent for that. Florence had two ideal visions of itself: It was the true inheritor of ancient Rome, eternal renown, wise republicanism; and it was also the city of God. Why else would the government insist that prostitutes dress as described in the Book of Isaiah? Why would there be talk of a crusade to bring the Holy Sepulchre to Florence? Centuries later, England would entertain the same delirium of piety *and* empire, producing that curious hybrid, the Christian gentleman. Some Americans still think these thoughts today, trying not to see the contradictions between Christian Puritanism and world domination.

Enamored of both visions, Cosimo attended regular discussions with Bracciolini, Niccoli, and other avant-garde humanists, and likewise regular meetings of the religious confraternity dedicated to the Magi. That he did sense a contradiction between political ambition and religious belief is evident from his famous remark, upon being accused of cruelty in exiling so many enemies, that "you can't run a state with paternosters." Christian charity takes the back seat when you're dealing with political necessity.

But contradictions, of course, were there to be overcome. That had always been Cosimo's attitude. And when it came to the conflicting claims of Christian devotion and secular fame, the most effective way to resolve the problem, as Cosimo had learned from the commissioning of Giovanni XXIII's tomb, was through art and architecture. "I know the Florentines," Cosimo told his bookseller and later biographer, Vespasiano da Bisticci. "Before fifty years are up we'll be expelled, but my buildings will remain." Most of those buildings were religious. You lavished money on the sacred, to gain earthly fame. *And* a place in heaven. Apparently you could have your cake and eat it too. Or have your wife drunk and the wine keg full, as the Italians say.

Having "accumulated quite a bit on his conscience," Vespasiano tells us, "as most men do who govern states and want to be ahead of the rest," Cosimo consulted his bank's client, Pope Eugenius, conveniently present in Florence (hence more or less under Cosimo's protection) as to how God might "have mercy on him, and preserve him in the enjoyment of his temporal goods." This was shortly after his return from exile.

Spend 10,000 florins restoring the Monastery of San Marco, Eugenius replied. It was the kind of capital required to set up a bank.

The monastery, however—a large, rambling, and crumbling structure within two minutes' walk of both the *duomo* and Cosimo's home—was presently run by a bunch of second-rate monks of the Silvestrine order reported as living "without poverty and without chastity." Unforgivable. I'll spend the money if you get rid of the Silvestrines and replace them with the Dominicans, Cosimo said. Those severe Dominicans! Only the prayers of men whose very identity was grounded in poverty and purity would be of use to a banker with an illegitimate child.

This was 1436, the year Pope Eugenius reconsecrated the *duomo* upon the completion, after more than fifteen years' work, of Brunelleschi's huge dome. With a diameter of 138 feet, the dome was the most considerable feat of architectural engineering for many hundreds of years. Its red tiles rose even higher than the white marble of Giotto's slender ornamental tower beside the cathedral's main entrance, and the two together completely dominated the skyline of the town in yet another ambiguous combination of local civic pride and devotion to faith. The Florentines, in fact, had for years been anxious that the dome would collapse, thereby inviting the ridicule rather than admiration of their neighbors.

On the occasion of the consecration, Cosimo bargained publicly with Eugenius to get an increase in the indulgence that the Church was handing out to all those who attended the ceremony. The pope gave way: ten years off purgatory instead of six. It cost no one anything and brought both banker and religious leader great popularity. On the matter of San Marco, the pope again proved flexible. The Silvestrines were evicted. The rigid Dominicans were moved in from Fiesole. Their leader at the time was Antonino, later Archbishop Antonino, a priest with a streak of fundamentalism about him. What would our Saint Dominic think, he wrote after the expensive renovation was complete, if he saw the houses and cells of his order "enlarged, vaulted, raised to the sky and most frivolously adorned with superfluous sculptures and paintings"?

But this fundamentalism was indeed only a streak—only a would-be severity, if you like—otherwise the priest could hardly have worked together with the banker for as long as he did. For the story of Cosimo's relationship with Antonino, who oversaw the lavish San Marco renovation project and then became head of the

Florentine church for most of Cosimo's period of power, is the story of the Church's uneasy accommodation with patronage of dubious origin. "True charity should be anonymous," Giovanni Dominici, founder of the Dominicans, had insisted. "Take heed," Jesus says, "that ye do not your alms before men, to be seen of them; otherwise ye have no reward of your Father which is in heaven." The position is clear: no earthly honor through Christian patronage. But Antonino and Cosimo were both sufficiently intelligent to preserve those blind spots that allow for some useful exchange between metaphysics and money: in the ambiguous territory of art. In return for his cash, the banker would be allowed to display his piety and power. And superior aesthetic taste. The Church would pretend that all this beauty was exclusively for the glory of God, as it readily pretended that the building of the *duomo*'s cupola had nothing to do with Brunelleschi's megalomania. Without such dishonesty, the world would be a duller place.

Michelozzo, more than ever Cosimo's personal friend after sharing his period of exile, was the architect. The monks' cells would be suitably austere. The library, with its rows of slim columns supporting clean white vaults, was a miracle of grace and light. Cosimo donated the books. Many were copied specifically for the purpose. Many were beautifully illuminated. The main artist in the project was Fra Angelico, otherwise known as Beato Angelico, a man who wept as he painted the crucifixions in all the novices' cells. Quarrel with that if you will. Antonino insisted on crucifixions, especially for novices. The true purpose of art is to allow the Christian to contemplate Christ's agony in every awful detail. But at the top of the stairs leading to those cold cells, Angelico's *Annunciation* presents two sublimely feminine figures generously dressed as if by Florence's best tailors. And in the church below, the monastery's main altarpiece, *The Coronation of the Virgin,* shows just how far Cosimo has come since the tomb of Giovanni XXIII.

Holding her unexpected child, the Virgin sits crowned with banker's gold in a strangely artificial space, as if her throne were on a stage, but open to trees behind. It was the kind of scene the city's confraternities liked to set up for their celebrations, funded of course by benefactors such as the Medici. Aside from San Marco and San Domenico (patron saints of the monastery and of its newly incumbent order), the figures grouped around the Holy Mother are *all* Medici name-saints: San Lorenzo, for Cosimo's brother, who had recently died; San Giovanni and San Pietro for Cosimo's sons. Kneeling at the front of the picture, in the finest crimson gowns of the Florentine well-to-do, are San Cosma and San Damiano. Cosma on the left, wearing the same red cap that Cosimo prefers, turns the most doleful and supplicating face to the viewer, the Florentine congregation. Apparently he mediates between the people and the Divine, as Cosimo himself had done the day he got the pope to hand out ten years' worth of indulgences instead of six. Damiano instead has his back to us and seems to hold the Virgin's eyes.

In later years, other managers of the Medici bank—Francesco Sassetti, Tommaso Portinari, Giovanni Tornabuoni—would have themselves introduced directly into biblical scenes. Solemn in senatorial Roman robes as they gazed on the holy mysteries, they

Fra Angelico's Coronation of the Virgin, *one of the many paintings commissioned by Cosimo de' Medici when he undertook the restoration of the monastery of San Marco. Six of the eight saints in attendance are Medici name saints, with St. Cosma turning to face the congregation in the foreground to the left, balanced by San Damiano on the right. Around the edge of the luxurious carpet run red balls on a golden field, the motif of the Medici family. The sacred space thus becomes more comfortable, for the rich.*

showed that at least in art there need be no contradiction between classical republic and city of God, between banker and beatitude. Cosimo had more tact. He appeared only by proxy, in his patron saint. Or saints. For he never forgot to include brother Damiano, perhaps half hidden by Cosma's body, turned toward the Virgin, or the crucifixion, as if half of the living Cosimo were already beyond this earth, in heaven, with his dead twin brother. No doubt this generated a certain pathos. "Cosimo was always in a hurry to have his commissions finished," said Vespasiano da Bisticci, "because with his gout he feared he would die young." He was in a hurry to finish San Marco, in a hurry to finish the huge renovation of his local church, San Lorenzo, then the beautiful Badia di Fiesole, the Santissima Annunziata, and many others as the years and decades flew by, including the restoration of the Church of the Holy Sepulchre in Jerusalem. Ever in a hurry, he grew old fearing he would die young. Perhaps it was this that made him such a master of the ad hoc.

WHEN THE RESTORATION of San Marco was finally finished in 1443, Pope Eugenius, now with his bags packed ready to return to a pacified Rome, agreed that the church should be reconsecrated under the name San Marco, San Cosma, and San Damiano. So Cosimo reminded everyone of his part in the project, but unobtrusively, as with the Good Men of San Martino. Not for him the gesture of the banker Giovanni Rucellai, who advertised his personal patronage by having his name written in yard-high letters right across the façade of Santa Maria Novella. All the same, an attentive observer would have noticed, in that San Marco altarpiece, a line of red balls around the lovely carpet on which the family name-saints knelt before the gorgeous Virgin. Were they really the red balls of the Medici family emblem? There were no *Last Judgments* in Cosimo's San Marco. Discreetly, head bowed and cap in hand, the profane invaded the sacred space and made it comfortable.

Cosimo practiced the banker's art of unobtrusive proximity. It wasn't enough that men dedicated to poverty had accepted his money and its role in their scheme of things, thus giving tacit approval to his business practices; they must also admit him right into their community, accept that he was one of them. So he had a cell built for himself beside the monks' cells. Except that Cosimo's cell had two rooms. It was larger and pleasanter. Over the door, engraved in stone, were the words of the papal bull that granted him absolution from all sins in return for his expenses. Few eyes would see this, but Cosimo wanted it written down, indelibly, like a bank contract that only the interested parties need consult. "Never shall I be able to give God enough to set him down in my books as a debtor," he remarked humbly of his huge outlay for San Marco. Yet clearly that was the kind of relationship he would have preferred.

Opposite the door of the first room of Cosimo's cell, on a wall that novices might glimpse as they walked along the corridor, was one of Fra Angelico's crucifixions. How could the monks not approve? But in the larger, private cell behind, with more expensive paints and stronger colors, Cosimo had the younger, more cheerful artist, Benozzo Gozzoli, assist Angelico in painting a procession of the Magi. It was Cosimo's favorite biblical theme. He

Gozzoli's Adoration of the Magi *(detail). Only in this fresco, painted around three walls of the tiny chapel in the heart of his great palazzo, did Cosimo at last allow himself to be depicted in a biblical scene. Typically unobtrusive, he wears black and rides a mule, while to his left (our right), son Piero is rather more magnificent on a white horse.*

would be responsible for at least half a dozen such pictures in his lifetime. All in bright colors. Fifteen years after San Marco, around three walls of the tiny chapel in the heart of his great *palazzo,* he and his son Piero had the same Gozzoli paint a lavish Magi procession in which, for the few who penetrated that sanctum, Cosimo himself at last appeared in person, riding on a mule behind the youngest of the three Magi. Common to many of the

Florentine elite, the Magi obsession is easily explained. What other positive images of rich and powerful men did the New Testament offer?

Cosimo's extension of his Church patronage beyond his own neighborhood and eventually all over town, the numerous depictions of Saints Cosma and Damiano, the raising of the Medici arms, the red balls on a golden field, in one sacred place after another—all this has been read, rightly no doubt, as the symbolism of political ambition. Certainly it caused resentment among those who felt their territory had been invaded, those exiles who lost their family chapels to members of the Medici clan.

The slow seeping of the sensual into sacred art, the more and more accurate depiction of the human form and the contemporary secular space, the growing physical beauty of the Madonna, the awareness of her breasts, her nipples even, the elegance of her long neck—all this has been understood as evidence of a new interest in everything earthly, a more positive humanist-inspired vision of our worldly lives. Rightly, no doubt. But there is more to it. There is magic.

What were the Magi if not magicians? They came to Jesus because that proximity was important to them. The gifts they brought had magical powers. Fourteen centuries later, the Florentines might be fascinated by money and material goods, but they hadn't reached the dull point where matter is *just* matter, or where symbolism is merely an artistic convention whereby abstract qualities can be evoked through this or that image. No, for the people of Cosimo's generation, a certain kind and color of dress, a particular hat, or a diamond ring still possessed powers that went beyond their being indicators of material wealth. Treated or processed in a certain way, material things could take on magical force. What was that rhinoceros horn doing in the Medici bank's warehouse, if not waiting to be ground up in a magic potion? The bones of a dead saint were also alive with magic. Keep them close and they will work miracles. To show reverence, to encourage the miracle, you put them in an elaborate reliquary, a work of the finest craftsmanship, of Ghiberti, or Donatello. Art and magic call to each other.

But alas, saints' bones are scarce. And rhinoceros horns even more so. When the great preacher, misogynist, and anti-Semite Bernardino di Siena died in 1444, the popular enthusiasm to possess some object that the charismatic man had touched left his poor donkey stripped of all those hairs that had rubbed the holy backside. Afterward, when the buying and selling began, how could you tell one donkey hair from another? How can you tell a real relic from a fake? The holy foreskin of our circumcised Lord is still held in one church in Italy. In 1352 the Florentine government had bought an arm of Santa Reparata from Naples, only to find it was made of wood and plaster.

But if you couldn't find or afford the saint himself, the real thing, there was always his painted or sculpted likeness. The faithful kissed the saint's stone feet, brushed his painted gown with theirs. They were *close* to him, through art. The banker Giovanni Rucellai had his tomb made in an *exact* likeness of the Holy Sepulchre. This mimicry could only make the passage to heaven easier. The copied image, that is, had a virtue that went beyond an aesthetic appreciation of the sensual world. It appropriated the

Donatello's reliquary bust of San Rossore (museum of S. Matteo, Pisa). Renaissance high art fuses with the miracle-working power of the saint's remains.

qualities of its model. It served to create proximity to the sacred. The craftsmanship of the reliquary and the power of the relic were fused together in the fine fresco that showed, convincingly, the saints about their miracles.

Fortunately, Cosimo had an eye for the gifted artist, as he had a nose for the trusty bank manager. Donatello might be a sodomist, but who else could make you feel you were so close to the Divine in bas-relief? His reliquary bust of San Rossore was the man himself in bronze. Fra Filippo Lippi might be a fornicator, liar, and cheat, but how *real* your patron saints were when painted in pride of place either side of the pure Virgin in the Church of Santa Croce. Cosma, Cosimo. The proximity of those names had meaning (all branches of the Medici bank observed a holiday on September 27, St. Cosma's Day). The cloak San Cosma wore in Lippi's painting was the same crimson as Cosimo's. He looked out at the devout viewer. The Virgin prayed for the saint, the saint for the viewer. Cosimo paid for prayers for the Florentines, prayers for his family, prayers for himself. Every day. The monks took the Medici bank's money, lived with the paintings, and prayed. A magical community had been formed—real, virtual, metaphysical. Pay, pray. This was the early Renaissance. *Pagare, pregare*. Wealth, devotion, and technique reconciled in the sorcery of art. Money rehabilitated. Antonino and Cosimo could get on.

Or perhaps not. "I invoke God's curse and mine on the introduction of possessions into this order." The words appear on a scroll held by a saint in another of Fra Angelico's depictions of the Virgin in San Marco, this time in a dormitory corridor where the only viewers would be the monks. Someone wasn't happy. Cosimo had asked for the restriction on bequeathing money to the Dominican order to be lifted, but the monks were resisting. They hadn't committed their lives to the severest of disciplines in order to grow rich. Was it right for a moneychanger to occupy such a position in their community? There was a sell-by date, it seemed, on much of what Cosimo did. Whether in the field of banking, or religious art, or politics, the magical balancing act, the expensive reconciliation of the irreconcilable, could last only so long.

IN 1438, HARD-PRESSED by the Turkish war machine, the leaders of the Eastern Church had come to Ferrara to see if they could resolve their doctrinal differences with the pope, accept his authority, and in return get help to raise the long siege of Constantinople. When Ferrara was hit by the plague, Cosimo took advantage to invite the Church leaders to Florence. Medici money brought the Orient to town, their strange clothes, their Greek manuscripts. Medici money paid for their lodgings, their food, their meeting places, as banking money today pays for so many well-meaning conferences.

Does the Holy Spirit proceed only from God the Father, as the Eastern Church maintained, or from both God the Father and God the Son, as Rome insisted? That was the issue under debate. It must have seemed child's play to a man used to the stubborn complexities of international trade. Surely one just decided, this or that. And after months of bitter dispute, the priests did in fact agree that Rome was right. Christendom rejoiced. Cosimo had played his part in resolving the schism that was the shame of every believer. But back in Constantinople, the Greek holy men were told they had exceeded their mandate, they had conceded too much, they had merely accepted the authority of the pope. The pact broke down. Even at the expense of annihilation, the Greeks didn't want to accept that they had got it wrong about the Holy Spirit. And if they persisted in such grave errors, Western Christendom could hardly be blamed if it left their eastern cousins alone against the mighty Turk. Even the most pious of bankers could do nothing about such determined integrity.

And there was very little Cosimo could do when the company of Giovanni Venturi and Riccardo Davanzati failed in Barcelona in 1447. Venturi & Davanzati, one of many Italian trading companies in Spain, had played a critical part in the process by which the Medici bank sought to keep money circulating among its various branches. The Barcelona company bought cloth from the Bruges branch of the Medici bank. The money it owed Bruges was then held in the Spanish city, to be drawn on by the Venice branch of the Medici bank to honor letters of credit issued to Venetian merchants who were importing saffron and Spanish wool. The merchant handed in his money to the Medici branch in Venice and Venturi & Davanzati paid it out to his suppliers in Barcelona. In this way, Bruges reduced its debt with Venice and with Italy in general.

But in the summer of 1447, the Spanish company was unable to honor 8,500 florins' worth of letters of credit. The Venetian merchants demanded their money back from the Medici. Bruges was left without payment for vast quantities of cloth and above all without a way of returning money to Italy. With the elaborate system of triangular trading on which the Medici bank depended becoming ever more precarious, the only solution now seemed to be to encourage Henry VI of England to accept loans in return for which he would allow the Medici to increase the amount of wool they were buying and sending to Italy. The loans would be repaid by exempting the Medici from export duties on whatever they bought.

It was a dangerous and expensive way of bringing money back to Italy, since it involved the constant concession of large amounts of credit. Medici managers set off for Contisgualdo (the Cotswolds) to watch the sheep shearing, then down to Antona (Southampton) to arrange for transport. With the monopoly of their own trade organization bypassed, the English wool merchants were furious. And many of the Florentine monks were likewise getting increasingly irritated about the number of bankers appearing in sacred paintings and demanding pride of place in their prayers. It seemed the more money you spent on those who wished to stay pure and poor, the greater the possibility of a fundamentalist backlash. Everywhere tension was building. In 1452 Girolamo Savonarola was born. Less than half a century hence, this fiery preacher would be running Florence and the Medici would have fled. Albeit briefly, the city of God would replace the Medici regime. In the political field as elsewhere, Cosimo's solutions always had a precarious feel about them.

THERE WAS A question that from time to time would form on the lips of the Florentine ruling elite: Should we admit such and such a person—a foreigner, an ambassador, a vulgar self-made man—into "the secret things of our town"? But surely, you object, in an open republic with a written constitution, there are no secrets, aside from military matters. What was this about?

On return from exile in 1434, Cosimo held no institutional position. He was a private citizen whose sentence had been revoked. He was the head of a triumphant faction taking power from another. Factions were illegal. The government, as we have seen, was elected by lot: at the top the *signoria,* which is to say eight priors and the *gonfaloniere della giustizia*. They proposed all legislation and held the powers of chief magistrates. Then the advisory bodies of the Sixteen Standard Bearers and the Twelve Good Men; then the Council of the People and the Council of the Commune, whose one power, but considerable, was that of a veto on legislation proposed.

What did Cosimo have to do with all this? What more could he be than another name in the leather bags from which, at staggered intervals, the *podestà*—a sort of mayor with no political power, usually a man from out of town—would select the members of the various government institutions, at random? The names in the bags were determined by a "scrutiny" held once every five years that assessed the male population on such criteria as age, wealth, family, guild membership, criminal record. On ousting the Medici in 1433, the Albizzi had held an unscheduled scrutiny to have the right sort of names put in the bags. Their great mistake had been not to eliminate the names of the previous scrutiny but merely to add new ones. Thus, with bad luck, it had happened that a pro-Medici *signoria* had been picked.

Whenever the process of government was stalled, when the

priors kept proposing as essential something the councils repeatedly vetoed as nefarious, then, as we recall, a parliament was called. The people flocked into the Piazza della Signoria and were bullied into conceding draconian powers. One says, "flocked," but in this archive-obsessed state, no accurate record was kept of the numbers of people in the piazza for a parliament. Nor of the way the vote split. It didn't split. This was an exercise of pure power, thinly dressed as democracy.

Why did the priors not call a parliament more often? Because the democratic rags were so very thin that not only did they fool no one, they didn't even allow people to *pretend* that they had been fooled. It had become important for the Florentines, as it is important for us today, to imagine that they shared, as equals, in a process of collective self-government. Should this patently not be the case for any extended period of time, then rebellion became legitimate. But as with the question, When is an exchange deal a loan with interest? or again, When is church patronage an expression of secular power? appearances, perceptions, definitions, and above all words were of the utmost importance. A coup d'état, for example, is called a parliament.

"The secret things of our town." The Florentines used the expression frequently, understood what it meant, and did not clarify. They did not clarify because they were referring to the embarrassing gap between the way things were supposed to be done and the way they were really done.

COSIMO RETURNS FROM exile. A parliament is held. It ratifies the formation of a *balia,* a large council that wields unlimited powers for a limited period. This is a wonderful equivocation. Unlimited power for a day can cast its shadow years hence. They could execute you. The *balia* confirms the sentences of those members of the Albizzi clan who have been exiled and announces more sentences. It invalidates the pro-Albizzi scrutiny of 1433 and orders the name tags it produced to be burned. It appoints a group of so-called *accoppiatori* to make a new scrutiny. *Accoppiatore* means "he who brings together"—he, that is, who couples the right names with the right bags, for some people will be suitable for serving on the Council of the Commune but not on the powerful *otto di guardia,* the commission of eight police chiefs. Some will be equipped for sitting on the city's public debt commission, but not for being governor of Pisa or Volterra.

Question: How can the priors, the *signoria,* be elected while the complex procedure of reviewing the whole male population to make the new scrutiny is carried out? Answer: The *accoppiatori*—Cosimo's inner circle—will stick just ten names, from Cosimo's inner and outer circle, into each election bag and the *podestà* will draw the government from those. This procedure, the *balia* ruled, was to last just a few months; *accoppiatore* is a temporary appointment. But the deadline for completing the scrutiny was put back—first to April 1435, then June, then October, then November, then March 1436. All in all, it was proving much easier to deal with a handful of names than with thousands.

In June 1436, the scrutiny is finally ready but the Councils of the People and of the Commune are persuaded to pass, *by a single vote,* a law that allows the priors to extend, for a year at a time, the right of the *accoppiatori* to prepare electoral bags with just ten names. And they do. For one year. Then another. It seems these shady civil servants have a regular job. *Accoppiatore* was beginning to take on the meaning "fixer." The priors extended their powers for a third year, at which point it was almost time for another scrutiny, though the names of the previous one have never really been used. But now there is a war on, and government finances are in desperate straits. This is not a time for the divisive business of scrutinizing the population and deciding who has a right to do what. Solidarity is at a premium. Month by month, election after fixed election, the *podestà*'s extractions of the priors' names are recorded in the city archives exactly as they always were since the constitution was first written. It is important to understand that all this is perfectly *legal*.

With uncanny good luck, Cosimo is elected *gonfaloniere della giustizia,* head of government, first immediately after his return from exile, then precisely as the heads of the Eastern Church arrive in Florence for their famous council of 1439, then again at a particularly tense moment in 1445. In short, he knows how to have his name pulled from the bag when it matters. But for the most part, Cosimo is careful to keep in the background, never to make a display of his unconstitutional power. "He mixed power with grace," Machiavelli tells us in his *Florentine Histories*. "He covered it over with decency." "And whenever he wished to achieve anything," says Vespasiano da Bisticci, "to avoid envy he gave the impression, as far as was possible, that it was they who had suggested the thing, not he."

Of course what the majority of people are suggesting to Cosimo is what kind of state or bank appointment they or their sons and grandsons and nephews would like to have. Begging letters pour in for positions that are supposedly chosen by lot. Cosimo does his best. But you can't please everyone. The Councils of the People and of the Commune are not happy. Is this Florentine republicanism? After the Battle of Anghiari in 1440, the defeat of Milanese troops and the consequent elimination of the Albizzi threat to the regime, the pressure of public opinion is such that the traditional system of truly random elections has to be restored.

But only for three years. In 1444 the ten-year sentence of exile on Cosimo's enemies is coming to an end. To have seventy old enemies return at once would be dangerous. So the councils are bullied into accepting a *balia,* thus once again temporarily conceding unlimited powers. The sentences of exile are extended for a further ten years. The electoral "experiments" resume.

In 1447 Visconti dies. With wonderful caprice, the duke bequeaths his title to Milan and all its territories not to Francesco Sforza, now married to his bastard daughter Bianca, but to Alfonso of Aragon, who had become king of Naples on defeating the Angevin family in 1442. Since the idea that the king of Naples in the extreme south should also possess Milan five hundred miles away in the far north was unthinkable to everybody except the man himself, the only possible reason for Visconti's doing this must have been to cause a maximum of confusion and resentment. And in fact, the people of Milan immediately reject the duke's will, rebel, and form a republic. The city's many subject towns take the opportunity of the ensuing power vacuum to declare independence. The Neapolitans march north into Tuscany with the intention of taking what is "legally" theirs. The Venetians march west toward Milan to capitalize on the chaos.

Furious, Francesco Sforza, who feels cheated out of his inheritance, joins the new republic in the fight to recapture its subject territories (and revenues) but then starts to claim them for himself whenever he is victorious.

Lombardy fragments. Over the next two years, all the major players will change sides at least once. So it is easy for the Medici regime to go on insisting that this is no time for erratic, randomly chosen governments. "The power of the *accoppiatori* was instituted to preserve the independence of Florence," Cosimo declares. Meantime, two questions obsess the endless consultative bodies (Cosimo's allies) poring over the electoral issue. First: Is a return to the constitutional system of random election ultimately inevitable to placate public opinion and republican sentiment? Second: If it is inevitable, can the *reggimento,* the status quo, somehow be guaranteed? "The greatest attention must be paid to *the technical aspects,*" announces Cosimo to one meeting. Whenever, in a democracy, we see our rulers obsessed with "the technical aspects" of the electoral process, whenever we see them tinkering with the size of constituencies, or machinery for counting ballots, then we know we are getting close to "the secret things of our town," the gap between respectable appearance and brutal reality. It would be rare for a banker not to be present.

THROUGHOUT THE 1440S and 1450s, draconian *balias* are instituted, made semi-permanent, then suddenly dissolved in the face of angry public reaction. New scrutinies are compiled with new rules. How many name tags are to be put in which electoral bags? How many members of the same family can serve on the same commission? Some people get only one tag in one bag and some get many tags in many bags. Some people are taxed out of business and some are hardly touched. "Whoever keeps in with the Medici does well for themselves," writes Alessandro Strozzi bitterly to his exiled brother-in-law. Again and again, the Councils of the People and of the Commune are presented with the most ambiguous legislation. They reject it. The *signoria* reformulates it. The regime is determined to follow the letter of the law, if rarely its spirit. The process is exhausting. Some of Cosimo's allies are calling loudly for a more drastic and definitive solution. They're losing patience. Why can't we have complete control and be done? But Cosimo has long since understood—and this is his modernity—that since power can no longer stem from a truly legitimate source, but is always at the end of the day "seized," it will always be at best ad hoc, pro tem. Any drastic and definitive solution would thus be a fort waiting to be stormed by someone else equally drastic and determined. It is better to appear to be in constant negotiation, constantly ready to compromise. In the end, the key thing is to keep people, if not actually happy, then happy *enough*. To keep the lid on.

The figure of the so-called *veduto* was important. When the *podestà* pulled a name from an electoral bag—for prior perhaps, or for one of the Twelve Good Men—the electoral officials had to check whether the person chosen wasn't in some way barred from holding office. Had he paid his taxes? Had he, or a member of his family, served in a similar office within the last two years? Was he presently resident in Florence? Was he, or any of his relatives, already sitting on another council or commission? In the old days, when the election really was an honest lottery, many names might be pulled from the bag before one was eligible. To be pulled from the bag was to be *veduto:* "seen." Actually to take office was to be *seduto:* "seated." Since the results of the scrutinies that decided which names were in which bags were kept secret, to be *veduto* for the position of prior—or, better still, *gonfaloniere della giustizia*—was a great honor. It meant you had passed the tough selection procedure, you were a respected citizen. When new consultative commissions were convened, being a *veduto* was often a criterion of eligibility.

With the new form of "elections"—just ten names in each bag, rather than hundreds—there had been no *veduti,* or very few. People were disappointed. Resuming control of the elections in 1443, after a brief return to the constitutional procedure, the *accoppiatori* began to arrange matters so that there would be plenty of *veduti, as if* the election had been carried out in properly random fashion. In short, they had names pulled out of the hat, names they knew were ineligible, not in order to take office but to be *veduti*. The trick was painfully obvious, but people were pleased all the same. They received an honor and were not burdened with responsibility. Such is the special humiliation of the fake democracy: the invitation to participate in farce. We have all sensed it. Cosimo, in fact, is creating a new kind of public figure: the person who declares his belief in the fairness of the system because it offers him a small sop, a public recognition. It treats him *as though he were an equal*. Among the eight priors, most of them Medici men who had served over and over again on all kinds of powerful commissions, there would often be one fellow who knew he was there for the only time in his life. A special favor. He would spend around a hundred florins, more than a year's salary perhaps, to buy the prior's expensive gown of saturated crimson; he would be feted and congratulated by all his relatives. But for the two months of his "power," he knew to ask no questions, nor to seek to influence decisions. From now on, he would always support the Medici. "Many were called to office," wrote one commentator, "but few were chosen to govern."

However secret the mechanisms by which the regime kept its grip on power, the results were now clear to everybody. A group of initiates from Cosimo's inner circle was fixing everything. And growing richer. Foreign ambassadors did their business at Cosimo's *palazzo,* rather than at the Palazzo della Signoria. The Milanese ambassador actually lived in Cosimo's house. Every decision required Medici consent. The man is a prince in everything but name, thought the other leaders in Italy. But there is a great deal in a name. Why else would princes worry so much about their coronations? Despite analogies, the Florentine citizen's condition was not quite the same as that of a subject in, say, the Papal States, or Milan. Equally powerless, he was mocked, or flattered, by the rhetoric of republicanism. He could not bow before his monarch in dignified fashion, saying, This is God's will, nor, alternatively, tell himself: This man is a usurper and I only bow down because brute force obliges me to. Why did he bow down, then? At the end of the day, the Councils of the Commune and of the People *did* still exist. They could veto legislation. Under the Medici, the Florentine mind was constantly fired by ideals of political freedom that were forever frustrated. A fizz of excited political thought frothed over the submerged reality of protracted dictatorship. If the war ever came to an end, a domestic show-down was inevitable.

IN THE PAY of the newly formed Republic of Milan, Francesco Sforza was fighting Venice. He also received money from the Medici bank. But the people of Milan soon realized that the *condottiere* was actually planning to take the city for himself. To defend themselves against him, they made peace with the Venetians behind Sforza's back. It wasn't enough. Sforza besieged the town, cut off its food supplies, and starved it into surrender. Quite simply, he was the most powerful military phenomenon in the area. Cosimo then shocked both Florence and the rest of Italy by being the first to give this bastard upstart official recognition as duke of Milan. Did he do it to secure the large amounts of money the bank had lent Sforza? Many members of Cosimo's own inner circle were angry and suspicious. Or was it because he honestly believed that further Venetian inroads into a weak Milanese republic would be a serious threat to Florence? Or for both reasons?

In any event, the Medici bank had already pulled its money and merchandise out of Venice before this momentous switch of alliances became known. There was nothing for the frustrated Venetians to seize in revenge. Outwitted, they sent agents to Florence to foment anti-Medici feeling. There was plenty of it. But when Venice allied itself with Naples for a joint attack on Florence and Milan, the Florentine people swung around behind Cosimo.

The key to unity in Italy is always the presence of a common enemy. "Never did a winning faction remain united, except when a hostile faction was active," says Machiavelli of the Florentines.

Ultimately, it was an enemy common to all of Italy that ended this new war just as it had begun to go rather badly for Florence. In May 1453, the Ottoman sultan Mehmet II captured Constantinople. Eastern Christendom had gone. At once the powerful Turks started to raid the Adriatic coast. It was a wake-up call of September 11 proportions. Time to stop quarreling. In 1454, the Peace of Lodi was signed and in 1455, with shameless rhetoric, a "Most Holy League" was declared, uniting Rome, Milan, Venice, Florence, and Naples against the Infidel. It thus turned out to have been a stroke of luck for Cosimo that the Greeks had been so stubborn about the nature of the Holy Spirit and found themselves alone against the tidal wave of Islam.

WITH THIS SUDDEN, unexpected peace, the political showdown in Florence could no longer be avoided. Their economy exhausted by the conflict, by another bout of the plague in 1448, and by an earthquake in 1453, many Florentines were starving. The councils insisted on a return to the old election by lot without the interference of the regime's *accoppiatori*. No sooner had they got what they wanted than a more neutral, less pro-Medici *signoria* introduced a property tax that seriously threatened the interests of the rich. Cosimo put on a brave face and said he approved of the tax. It was important for him to have support from the lower orders. His fellow travelers were not so pleased.

Prominent men were having to sell property to pay the tax. Still unsatisfied, the councils now also wanted a new, free, and fair scrutiny, which would mean more anti-Medici names in the electoral bags. What would happen if the government were really chosen at random after an impartial assessment of those qualified to serve? Where would the Medici be then?

Nervous, the regime seized on the chance of a favorable *signoria* to ask the councils to grant unlimited powers again. They would not. Since members of the councils cast their votes (actually beans) secretly, it was hard to twist their arms. When the legislation was sent back for the nth time, the priors demanded that votes be cast openly. The *signoria*'s two-month term of office was running out. At this point, Archbishop Antonino got involved on the councils' side and threatened the regime's bullies with excommunication if they tried to alter the constitution in this way. Perhaps precisely because the Church had taken so much money from the Medici, it felt the need to declare its independence. Voting in secret, the Council of the Commune and the Council of the People again rejected the proposed legislation. They were determined to bring rhetoric and reality together. Florence must be governed as the constitution stipulated. They wanted freedom.

This was the summer of 1458. As a last resort, the pro-Medici priors of the *signoria* decided to call a parliament, the first since 1434. Cosimo's consent was sought and given. But first they waited until the Milanese ambassador had convinced Sforza to dispatch troops to Florence. With soldiers from Milan in place at all entrances to the piazza, the parliament went as parliaments must. Old, tired, and chronically ill, Cosimo was careful not to attend.

A new, hundred-strong council was formed with complete power over all "matters of security." It was a permanent *balia,* but without the dangerous name. From that point on, the pretense of legality was pure formality: a limited group of men would go on electing each other to this or that body without fear of interference. You could join in, but only if you were willing to toe the Medici line. Any real opposition would have to be armed. No one had the stomach for it. If this was a success for the regime, it was certainly a defeat for Cosimo, who had much preferred the pleasant façade, the collusion of grateful clients, the satisfaction of having persuaded people to do something that he had never openly requested. But the tools of persuasion that make such things possible today—our modern media, mass production, and mass consumption—were not available to the Medici. Nor had anybody thought of the trick of allowing two apparently opposing but secretly complicitous factions to rotate in power at the whim of a complacently "enfranchised" population. The strategy of the two-party democracy lay far away in the future. Meantime, Cosimo was growing more and more preoccupied with the prospect of life after death, and friends were becoming rivals.

At the Medici bank's head office, Giovanni Benci was dead. Cosimo's younger and favorite son, Giovanni, proved a poor replacement. He preferred the high life to the calculation of profit and loss. Immoderately fat, he bought himself a nice slave girl while serving as ambassador to the Curia in Rome. It was becoming a family tradition. Disappointed, Cosimo brought home the Geneva director, Francesco Sassetti, one of the world's all-time great flatterers, to work beside his son. It was a sign the old banker was losing his grip. Sassetti wasn't up to it. Having achieved his position through servility, he was incapable of imposing discipline. A branch was opened in Milan, but like the venture in Ancona years ago, it was mainly there to serve Sforza. There was very little serious trade in and out of Milan and hence little chance of profits from exchange deals. While a bank benefited an economy doing business—an economy such as Venice, for example—there was nothing it could do in Milan but encourage a duke to spend more than he ought.

Still, at least Italy was mostly at peace, and Cosimo was taking a lot of the credit for it. His astuteness, if it was that, lay not so much in his having switched Florence's alliance from Venice to Milan as in having reduced the number of major players in the political game to match the number of states available. Anchored in Milan, Sforza was no longer a loose cannon, a military power without a state. Hence he no longer needed to fight to have an income. Cosimo hadn't quite foreseen the consequences of this. He had expected Sforza would help Florence conquer Lucca in exchange for all the Medici money that had been showered on him in his struggle to become duke. Perversely, Sforza hung up his sword and settled down with wife and nineteen children, legitimate and otherwise, to enjoy his earthly possessions.

FREQUENTLY BEDRIDDEN, Cosimo no longer accepted public office. His sons, themselves middle-aged, were sick too. They all suffered from gout. When not away at their country estates, all three had to be carried around the huge *palazzo* they had built in town, among their beautiful collections and possessions. Cosimo cried in pain when he was lifted. There was a problem with urine retention. Taking a keen interest in Plato's ideas about eternal life, paying generously for a new translation of the complete works of the philosopher, he now did most of his business in the windowless, candlelit chapel at the heart of the Palazzo Medici. On the walls, Gozzoli's wonderful *Journey of the Three Kings* glimmered all around, showing Cosimo and his family beside the Magi, their donkeys carrying heavy merchandise across distant landscapes, rather as if bank and Bible had got mixed up. There was a monkey, too, sitting on a horse, and a cheetah. The bank occasionally dealt in exotic animals. Archbishop Antonino, who had not in the end excommunicated anyone over the 1458 coup, made a point of condemning supposedly sacred pictures that distracted the viewer's attention with frivolities. He explicitly mentioned monkeys and cheetahs. Such is an established church's opposition to the regime it lives with.

Cosimo heard mass. Above the altar, there was Lippi's lovely painting of the Virgin and Child, plus a reliquary with genuine fragments from Our Lord's passion. Hard to come by. And to make the man feel even safer, there was a secret tunnel to escape through—to be carried through, that is—should anyone ever have the nerve to try the frontal assault. It was in this tiny chapel that Cosimo received the men of the regime, to discuss "the secret things of our town." It was in the chapel that Francesco Sforza's son, Galeazzo, found him in 1459. Likewise, the marquis of Mantua's son in 1461. On the second occasion, both Cosimo and Piero were in too much pain from their gout to give the youngster a tour of the great house. Only Giovanni was mobile. Limping heavily, his arm hanging on a servant's neck, the obese man insisted he would oblige, but gave up when it came to tackling the stairs. Money and magic were impotent here. Moving goods all over Europe, the Medici men rarely made it to the top floor.

Giovanni died in 1463. Depressed, Cosimo knew he was next. Burial arrangements were carefully negotiated. No doubt money changed hands. He would lie beneath the very center of the nave of the Church of San Lorenzo, in close proximity to the relics of the holy martyrs. Above the sarcophagus, a stone column would connect it to the tomb-marker on the church floor, a large white porphyry circle enclosing two crossed oblongs, a magical motif signifying, apparently, eternity. The effect, when one visits San Lorenzo today, is both unobtrusive and absolutely central: the banker's vocation. Barely noticed, he is the ground beneath the communicant's feet. A last generous endowment paid for a mass to be said for Cosimo's soul 365 days a year in perpetuity, and quality funeral clothes for all the mourners, including four female slaves. It is the only news we have of them.

5

Blue Blood and White Elephants

During the hot days and nights of August 1466, an old drama played itself out in the streets and *palazzi* of Florence. Once again the city was divided into two armed camps. Once again a transfer of power was in the air. Yet the principal actors seemed strangely hesitant, as if reluctant to rehearse what had been done so many times before, or unsure perhaps as to how to proceed in these different times.

Cosimo had died and something had to change. "With Cosimo your plan is impossible," the exiled Palla Strozzi had told Girolamo Machiavelli when the rebel came looking for support to overturn the banker's regime. "Without him it will be unnecessary." Cosimo was revered *and* he had had the money. Members of other old and wealthy families addressed him as "father." Still, they had built the regime *with* him, they told themselves, not *for* him. And certainly not for his son. Piero had no hereditary right, no special charisma, nor perhaps so much money. The bank was in difficulty. Banks in general were in difficulty. So while in 1458 the challenge to the

Medici had been launched through legal institutions, in line with the constitution, it now came, more seriously, from Cosimo's ex-partners in the regime—the ones who for decades had manipulated the constitution on his behalf. Suddenly, four canny old men were talking about liberty.

Dietisalvi Neroni, one of Cosimo's oldest collaborators and brother of the city's new archbishop, had been annoyed when plans to expand the Medici *palazzo* threatened to take light away from his own. Such a slight would clearly be perceived as a comment on his diminishing importance. Immediately after Cosimo's death, Neroni wrote to Francesco Sforza in Milan that just as Cosimo had been a father to other members of the *reggimento,* so they would now be fathers to Piero—i.e., the Medici are no longer the leading family. This is an oligarchy, not a principality.

Agnolo Acciaiuoli, like Cosimo, had been exiled in the 1430s for his opposition to Rinaldo degli Albizzi and had been in the Medici regime from the beginning. But in 1463 Acciaiuoli's daughter-in-law abandoned her husband Raffaello. He preferred boys and old Agnolo was violent, she complained. She wanted her dowry back. Being a Bardi girl, this was big money, 8,500 florins. Called in to arbitrate, Cosimo had said the young wife should be guaranteed her dowry, after which she could decide of her own free will whether or not to return to her husband. Agnolo was not happy with this. And he was particularly unhappy when Cosimo, having promised that another son of his, Lorenzo Acciaiuoli, would be given the next available bishopric in Tuscany, in the event preferred his own relative, Filippo de' Medici, when that bishopric turned out to be in the sensitive subject town of Pisa.

"Cosimo and Piero are cold men," Agnolo wrote in one of many letters to Duke Francesco Sforza. "Sickness and age have made them such cowards that they run away from everything that bothers them or requires any effort." Ever since Milanese troops had presided over that parliament of 1458, everybody, it seemed, was eager to present himself to Sforza as the next leader of the regime.

Everybody except Luca Pitti. Pushing seventy, Pitti had always been one of the most authoritarian and antidemocratic members of Cosimo's coterie. As *gonfaloniere della giustizia,* he personally had called the 1458 parliament that put an end to republican opposition. He had suffered no slights from the Medici family, but as an extremely wealthy banker in the process of completing a *palazzo* that was intended to surpass any in town, Luca had no intention of bending a knee to anyone now that Cosimo was gone. In November 1465, when Piero de' Medici insisted that he had Sforza's blessing for running Florence, Pitti replied that he would rather be governed by the devil than by Milan. All at once he became the figurehead of an opposition, which, however, didn't seem entirely consistent on foreign policy.

Niccolò Soderini, the fourth man, the most charismatic, may indeed have been a fervent republican. Or perhaps all he wanted was to reorganize those electoral bags to guarantee an upper-class oligarchy in which no single family would dominate. The Florentine patriarchy had always loathed Cosimo's sly habit of bringing in "vile new men" who gave him a power base beyond and potentially opposed to the older families' interests. Niccolò may also have resented the fact that his younger brother, Tommaso Soderini, was a major figure in the Medici faction. As always in

Florence, there was a thick web of family relations straining this way and that. Cosimo, for example, had always thought Agnolo Acciaiuoli a bad influence on his (Cosimo's) nephew, Pierfrancesco de' Medici, who was married to Agnolo's daughter Laudamia. Pierfrancesco was important; as the only son of Cosimo's brother Lorenzo, he held fifty percent of the Medici stake in the whole bank, though he didn't work for the bank or seek important roles in government. With Cosimo's death, Pierfrancesco was theoretically an equal partner with Piero. Having spent a great deal less on gathering allies about him, he possessed a great deal more ready cash.

NOW THAT HE was gone, it soon became clear how much Cosimo had relied on consensus for his authority. The special powers of the eight police chiefs, the so-called *otto di guardia,* were due to lapse. Piero wanted them renewed. The old men of the regime opposed him. The powers were not renewed. Piero wanted the *accoppiatori* to keep choosing a safe, pro-Medici *signoria*. The old men insisted on a return to random election. They had their way. And surprise, surprise, the first randomly chosen *gonfaloniere della giustizia* was Niccolò Soderini, one of the four. His two-month spell of government in late 1465 achieved nothing, but it left the town aware of being radically split. "We have divided the earth," Acciaiuoli would later say, "and division breeds leaders, leaders get nervous."

Piero had every reason to be nervous. Taking over the bank from Cosimo, he had found it undercapitalized, overstretched. He called in debts. Was it his covert enemy Dietisalvi Neroni who advised him to do this? In *Florentine Histories,* Machiavelli claimed it had been a ruse on Neroni's part to make Piero unpopular. Successful godfathers do not resort to credit squeezes. Many companies failed. People were resentful. All at once the Palazzo Medici was attracting fewer petitioners. Everybody was paying respects to Luca Pitti in his even-grander *palazzo*. A rival mesh of patronage was gaining ground.

Then in March 1466, with exquisite bad timing, Francesco Sforza died. The duke's wife and son immediately begged the Florentine *signoria* for a loan of 60,000 florins to pay for the military presence that would guarantee the Sforza family's succession throughout Milan's subject territories. Dietisalvi Neroni and Agnolo Acciaiuoli immediately changed position on Milan. After years of currying Sforza's support, they now would not give a loan to his successors, who, of course, represented Piero's potential army.

The slide accelerates. In May 1465, four hundred leading citizens of Florence swear and sign an oath to uphold the old republican system of government with election by lottery. Piero's cousin, Pierfrancesco de' Medici, signs. Has he been pushed to make the gesture by his Acciaiuoli wife, his persuasive father-in-law? Does he perhaps believe the bank would do better if it retreated from politics? The reasons can hardly matter to Piero. He is so paralyzed by gout these days that there are times when the only thing he can move is his tongue. His main business partner is undermining him. Everybody can see how weak he is.

Then in June 1465, the government starts debating the dissolution of the so-called Council of 100, the permanent *balia* of Medici men set up after the 1458 parliament to ratify everything the Medici governments wanted. With its departure, the return to the old constitution will be complete and the family's power at an end. The change that Palla Strozzi foresaw after Cosimo's death is at hand. Piero is beaten, unless . . . unless he himself can bring about a different kind of change, a metamorphosis of the family and its relationship with the other patriarchal families in the regime. In this long and no doubt suffocatingly hot Tuscan summer, political emergency accelerates a trend that has been underway for decades, and at last creates something new.

THE REAL SCANDAL of money, as we have already said, is that it does not respect traditional hierarchies. The merest artisan can make a fortune and start strutting around in expensive crimson. The feudal order breaks down. But once made, money notoriously seeks that which cannot—supposedly—be bought. Perhaps the first generation is happy to have acquired material wealth, but the second yearns for a distinction that is not based on money, a distinction that in the past only birth could give. In the end, the individual, even the richest, resists the idea that his worth is to be quantified in money terms, especially if it wasn't he who earned the cash. So we come back to Achilles's conviction that human uniqueness has no price, and we arrive at the roots of every snobbery: I wish to be distinguished, but how?

Education is a good place to start. Money buys it and it then generates a value that goes beyond money. Art achieves the same alchemy. "Money alone," remarked the wondering Galeazzo Sforza (Francesco's son), when shown around the art treasures of the Palazzo Medici, "would not be able to compete with what has been done here." Yet everything had been bought with money.

What was the proper education for a rich banker? Giovanni di Bicci had done no more than follow fashion when he gave Cosimo his humanist tutors. Steeped in Cicero, the young man was seduced by the ideal of the noble leader. He wanted to be such a man. The Florentine constitution, with its system of election by lottery, forbade these ambitions, yet was so weak that it more or less invited a rich man to spend his way to an ambiguous, covert sort of power. If one of the huge problems of any democracy is what to do with big money and its attendant political ambitions, squalid or noble, Florence had clearly got it wrong.

No doubt aware of the many conflicts within himself, between private and public interest, between moneymaking and getting to heaven, Cosimo decided to educate his three sons for different and separate careers. Piero, the eldest, would be groomed for government; Giovanni, the favorite, for the bank; Carlo, the illegitimate boy with the foreign features, could go to the Church. It was as if the three strands of Cosimo's achievements could be separated out. Though Cosimo's genius had lain in intertwining those strands.

Carefully laid, the plans made no allowance for character and circumstance. Carlo was happy enough as a bishop, but fat Giovanni couldn't get excited about banking. Jolly, well loved, and vain, he chose the peacock as his personal emblem. "For the view," he explained to Cosimo, who couldn't understand why his son was building a villa in Fiesole with no agricultural land around it. A villa was always a farmhouse for Cosimo. You give your children an expensive education and their values start to shift. Cosimo should have been ready for this, since his own education had led to radical departures from his father's lifestyle.

Determined to please, perhaps precisely because he was not the favorite, Piero was most at home overseeing Cosimo's commissions of buildings and works of art. An avid collector, in love with lavish furnishings and beautiful domestic interiors, he would spend hours gloating over stacks of illuminated manuscripts, or collections of antique coins. He slept on silk sheets embroidered with the family coat of arms. But you must train for government, his father insisted. And train Piero dutifully did. He held a number of government posts: prior, *accoppiatore,* even *gonfaloniere della giustizia*. As his personal emblem, he chose the falcon, which always returns faithfully to its master. "Honored, like your father," was how people addressed him in their begging letters. "A most careful imitator of his father's admirable virtues," wrote Donato di Neri Acciaiuoli in a dedicatory preface to his *Life of Hannibal and Scipio Africanus*. But imitate as he might, Cosimo's role wasn't available to Piero. Because Cosimo hadn't succeeded anyone.

Accusations that Cosimo had been eager to become a prince were off the mark. He thrived on the complications, the ambiguities, the idea that his fellow Florentines had elevated him *despite* the constitution. Florence had stripped its feudal nobles of their privileges and didn't want a return to the past. Yet education was breeding aristocratic presumptions in the banker's children. Their life began to resemble that of noblemen. Is it possible, they must have started to wonder, to *invent* an aristocracy, a new, more sophisticated version of the crude old birthright—not simply and brutally to seize power but to create, over two or three wealthy and well-read generations, a new hereditary privilege?

The future of Europe for centuries to come would depend on the answer to this question. And that answer, of course, is no. Money and culture do *not* amount to a divine right to pass on political power to one's heirs. And yet . . . if sufficiently enlightened, if supported by effective propaganda, if interminably intermarried with others who had similar pretensions, or who had once been recognized as royal, perhaps the world might be convinced by an expensive parody, an ersatz aristocracy—especially if, at the end of the day and in the teeth of the evidence, the people enjoying the privileges were always willing to declare themselves ordinary citizens. Paralyzed on silk sheets through the summer of 1466, Piero de' Medici could hardly be likened to a chrysalis turning into a butterfly. But before the year was out, he would have freed the Medici family from the sticky limitations of the old Florentine oligarchy. With wings bought from usury, the Medici bankers would soar above their station at last. The gouty man was plotting a marriage that would turn those republicans green with envy.

Like art and education, marriage was something that involved an exchange of money but also had the potential for distinctions that went beyond money. These are the interesting things in life, where countable and uncountable values rub and spark together. Traditionally, it was the bride who had to purchase, with her dowry, the right to her husband's protection. Piccarda de' Bueri's 1,500 florins had been crucial for husband Giovanni di Bicci's initial investments. The Bueri were solid Florentine merchant stock; no more. A distant cousin of Piccarda's would serve thc Medici bank as an agent in Lubeck, collecting papal dues from Scandinavia; trading in furs, amber, and linen; keeping all his accounts in Italian to baffle the local taxman.

But a future husband, or his negotiating parents, also had the option of accepting less money in return for more prestige. Her branch of the family being out of luck, Contessina de' Bardi didn't bring Cosimo much cash, but she was still a Bardi. It was a valuable alliance. The wife chosen for Cosimo's son, Piero, Lucrezia Tornabuoni, brought even less money, a mere 1,000 florins, but in return for even more prestige. Once aristocratic, Lucrezia's family had changed its name from Tornaquinci to Tornabuoni to avoid the ban on noblemen participating in public life. The girl had blue blood. How strange that the Florentines had banned the nobles from exercising political power but were still impressed by their pedigrees. Many modern democracies are still tensed by this contradiction. Lucrezia, however, legitimized her special status by being nobly educated as well as nobly born. But can one really say, "nobly educated"? Doesn't such an expression mean we've accepted the premise that education can buy certain rights? In any event, Lucrezia was well read. She wrote devotional poetry, of the kind sung by religious confraternities. She made her own small venture into business, redeveloping some rundown sulfur baths, no doubt with her menfolk's gouty joints in mind.

Accepting Piero's illegitimate daughter, Maria—these little trials came with the territory—Lucrezia produced two daughters, Bianca and Lucrezia, and two sons, Lorenzo and Giuliano. Most of all, she presided over Lorenzo's extremely noble education and, when his turn came, played an important role in choosing his wife. With Piero's health so feeble, Lorenzo would have to marry young, while the family still had clout. In Rome, Medici banking agents were already negotiating for the hand of an Orsini. This was a family of feudal lords, cardinals, *condottieri*. A family with a private army, no less. Inevitably, news of the possible marriage fed the Florentine opposition. Why was Piero looking outside his hometown for his son's wife? People started complaining, remarks Machiavelli, "that he who does not want citizens as relatives wants them as slaves." Before bankers and feudal lords could mix, Piero de' Medici would have to survive this dangerous summer of 1466.

IN BED, Piero calls for lists to be made of those for him, those against. Interestingly, the two lists include many of the same names. It's a good sign: minds are malleable, or susceptible to patronage perhaps. In late August, the sick man precipitates the crisis. An ambush, he claims, was laid to murder him as he was being carried toward Florence in a litter from the family villa in Careggi. The assassins were troops of Borso d'Este, marquis of Ferrara. Could this be true? They were in the pay of Luca Pitti and Agnolo Acciaiuoli. So Piero claims. Anyway, he is taking up arms in response. Suddenly, the whole Medici countryside to the north of the town is on the move. Two thousand Milanese troops are approaching from Bologna. And I need 10,000 florins, Piero tells his business partner and cousin Pierfrancesco. At once!

Despite having sworn that oath to defend the republic, Pierfrancesco obeys. Why? Does he believe this unlikely assassination story? Is he afraid that if Piero were to be murdered, the bank might collapse? Whatever the reason, he produces this vast sum at once, in cash. Hours later, all the bread, wine, and arms in the town have been bought up. These provisions are a magnet to the waverers. Scaffolding appears around the Palazzo Medici, creating vantage points from which to pelt attackers. The nearest city gate is seized to allow friendly troops to enter. So much for the coward who would run away from everything that required effort.

The opposition is thrown. They are indeed in alliance with Borso d'Este of Ferrara, but can they get the *condottiere* and his army into the town before the Milanese arrive? Are they willing to put their hands in their pockets, or other people's, as deeply and drastically as Piero has? They hesitate. To arms, Niccolò Soderini insists. They must ride through the streets, now, rousing the common people who are doubtless on their side. They must attack Piero's house. There is no time to lose. But what, the others ask, if the people, after winning, want real power? What if, having sacked Piero's *palazzo,* the plebs start attacking other *palazzi*? In the middle of the night, armed men bang on the gates of the Palazzo Medici. Panic spreads among Piero's defenders. It's only Antonio Ridolfi, another supporter come to join them. The opposition has missed its moment. It is never enough just to have money—the Strozzi family, for example had had more money than the Medici in 1433, and they were still in exile—you must know how to use it when it matters. Above all, you can never afford to be tight.

Piero staged this melodrama on August 27, one day before a new *signoria* was to be elected, by lot. Was this because he feared that he would need to be armed if the draw went against him? Or because he had fixed the election somehow and knew it would be in his favor? As it turned out, the new *signoria* was decidedly pro-Medici. Fixed or not, nothing could have demonstrated more clearly the need for a less erratic form of election.

There is now a four-day interregnum before one *signoria* hands over to another. The city is surrounded by foreign troops, from both sides. Anything could happen. Negotiations begin. To discourage rash decisions, Piero makes promises. Behind the scenes, the Medici bank's general director, Francesco Sassetti, goes to talk to the aging Pitti. Time to change sides, Luca. And Pitti, the figurehead of the opposition, betrays his friends in exchange for three guarantees: the promise of a position as *accoppiatore* for himself; the appointment of his brother to the *otto di guardia* (with the power over exile); and the marriage of his daughter Francesca to "someone very close to Piero." By whom Pitti believes they mean Piero's eldest son and heir, Lorenzo.

A few days later—and this is a coup within the coup—it is Luca Pitti, not Piero de' Medici, who proposes the inevitable "parliament." Two thousand Milanese troops preside. Joining them, armed and on horseback, is Piero's son, the seventeen-year-old Lorenzo. It's quite a show. In very short order, all the regime's old electoral controls are reintroduced. And more. Seeing the makeup of the new police commission, which once again has special pow-

Ghirlandaio's Birth of John the Baptist *(detail), in Santa Maria Novella (Tornabuoni chapel). Acting on instructions from Giovanni Tornabuoni, the painter seems more interested in his portrayal of these fifteenth-century spectators—the women of the Tornabuoni family—than in the biblical scene itself. The older of the two women wearing white headscarves is Lucrezia Tornabuoni, Lorenzo's mother.*

ers, Dietisalvi Neroni, Niccolò Soderini, and Agnolo Acciaiuoli flee the city before the inevitable sentence of exile is passed. If the 1458 crisis served to define the relationship between the regime and the institutions, the 1466 parliament settled the Medici's position within the regime: total domination.

Despised and ignored, the turncoat Luca Pitti got his position of *accoppiatore* as promised, and with his brother on the Eight of the Guard, he was spared exile. But his young daughter, Francesca, did not get to marry Lorenzo. Instead she was given to Lorenzo's uncle, Piero's brother-in-law, the thirty-six-year-old Giovanni Tornabuoni, head of the Medici bank in Rome and already well advanced in negotiations to bring that Orsini girl to Florence for his nephew.

"She walks with her head a little stooped," complained Lucrezia Tornabuoni. A bare six months after the political crisis, Lorenzo's mother was down in Rome to size up her future daughter-in-law. "I believe this comes from shyness." Did the child have breasts? "Hard to tell the way these Romans dress." Anyway, "as well as half of Monte Ritondo," Lucrezia writes home to Piero, "the family also owns three other castles and . . . are better off every day because, apart from being maternal nephews of the Cardinal, of the Archbishop Napoleone, and of the knight, they are also related as cousins via their father for he is second cousin to the aforesaid Lords who love them greatly." This was what mattered. The girl was sixteen. Oh, her name is Clarice, the future mother-in-law remembers to say halfway through a second letter. Only eighteen, Lorenzo was taken down south to view the goods and said they would do. The Medici were about to move into a different class. The trend behind that move would be the ruin of the bank.

"THIS COMPANY USED to promote everyone who was good at his job, without any regard to family or privilege." Back in 1453, Leonardo Vernacci, deputy director of the Rome branch, had written to Giovanni di Cosimo, then deputy director of the Medici holding, to complain about the promotion of Giovanni Tornabuoni. Tornabuoni had joined the company at the age of fifteen in 1443, the same year Piero di Cosimo married his sister, Lucrezia Tornabuoni. Vernacci accused young Giovanni of slacking. Now he was being promoted over the head of the talented young Alessandro Bardi, who quit as a result. Tornabuoni wrote to his sister's husband, Piero (not to Giovanni), to complain about the complaints. "And Vernacci spies on me and reads my post!" In 1465 it would be Vernacci who now left the bank in disgust when Piero promoted his brother-in-law to the directorship of the Rome branch.

Giovanni Tornabuoni had no special talents; he was obstinate, touchy, and self-important, but as a relative of the family he did appear in that Magi procession that Benozzo Gozzoli painted in the chapel in the Palazzo Medici, and later in life he actually commissioned a number of fine frescoes himself—first in Rome, when the young wife whom Luca Pitti had given him died in 1477, and again back in Florence in Santa Maria Novella, where the painter Ghirlandaio depicted a now-elderly Tornabuoni and his friends and relatives in decidedly patriarchal poses. Here the religious themes, in a fresco such as *The Angel Appearing to Zacharias,* fade discreetly into the background, while the senatorial figures of the contemporary Florentines in their robes and caps dominate the scene in what is now almost a work of journalism.

In *The Birth of John the Baptist,* the Tornabuoni women stand center stage, entirely displacing the biblical scene to show off their modern, carefully tailored clothes and clearly identifiable household jewelry. It is an arrogant though always elegant parody of the early days of Cosimo's church patronage, where at best a banker might creep into the frame through his name-saint. If the frescoes of San Marco in the 1430s made the sacred space a little less forbidding, a little more breathable for the busy dealer in dry exchanges, in the Tornabuoni Chapel in Santa Maria Novella that space has been unequivocally commandeered, utterly confused with the world of the contemporary Italian patrician. But then, as director of the Medici bank in Rome, Giovanni had spent his entire adult life in a papal court increasingly concerned with luxury, prestige, and power, not theology. And the irony is that the more worldly the Church became, the *less* attractive it was for bankers like Tornabuoni—as a customer, that is. The cost of the papal bureaucracy was soaring (500 employees had become 2,000), the price of nepotism likewise. Not to mention the expansionist wars. From the 1460s onward, the Medici bank was lending out more to the Curia than it was taking in with the commission on papal tributes. All too soon, the classic situation would be reached where the indebted client has the upper hand, the bank is too deeply involved to pull out.

Another man painted together with the Medici family in Gozzoli's famous Magi procession was Francesco Sassetti, who had been appointed deputy general director of the bank's holding in 1453, when Giovanni di Cosimo clearly was not pulling his considerable weight in the top position. Like Tornabuoni, Francesco

Sassetti married an upper-class fifteen-year-old when in his late thirties, and again like Tornabuoni he had Ghirlandaio paint him (standing beside Lorenzo de' Medici) for his family chapel, this time the Church of Santa Trinità. Was this a competition? If the Medici were to become aristocrats through marriage, education, and patronage, those around them clearly assumed that they themselves must take on a greater importance too.

A change now occurred in the bank's structure that would eventually allow this trend to get out of hand. Whenever one of the parties involved in a company contract died, the contract was dissolved. As general manager of the Medici holding in the halcyon years from 1443 to 1455, Giovanni Benci had been signatory to all the company's branch contracts; hence, on his death, *all* the bank's contracts had to be rewritten. At this point, the idea of the holding company was dropped. There is no letter or report to explain this fatal decision. From now on, the Medici share in each branch of the bank would be held *directly* by members of the family in partnership with the local managers and not through the holding. This meant that the general manager of the bank as a whole—when not a Medici, and it would never again be a Medici—no longer had a personal, financial interest in each separate branch through his share in the holding. Francesco Sassetti, for example, who held the top position for most of the rest of the bank's life, from 1458 to 1490, only had shares in the Avignon and Geneva branches. As far as he personally was concerned, all the others could run at a loss. And during the three decades of his leadership, most of them did. Dramatically. At the same time, Sassetti himself became extraordinarily rich. By 1462, aside from house, farms, jewels, and other valuables, he had built up a fortune of 45,000 florins. All made with the bank. Four years later, in a period in which the bank was losing heavily, that fortune had gone up to 97,000 florins, enough to start a major bank of his own. It included large sums of money held in "discretionary" (interest-bearing) Medici accounts under such names as "The Convent of the Celestini," or "a friend in Florence." And since everyone had now understood that a show of learning reinforced claims to nobility, Sassetti had built up a library too, a very considerable library. In each book was a bookplate with his name and the little motto: *À mon pouvoir* (in my power . . .).

Yet one thing that was never in Sassetti's power were the decisions of the Medici bank's distant branches, decisions that he was supposed to be coordinating. Part of the problem, no doubt, was that without the holding system, he felt no pressing personal need to bring those branches into line. But this state of affairs was exacerbated by the fact that the branches' managers now shared Sassetti's and the Medici's aspirations to grandeur. "Most of them do what they want," Sassetti complained, "with no regard, and take too much freedom." What these men were mostly doing was lending far too much of the bank's money to the people they wished to spend time with and resemble: kings, princes, dukes, lords, and cardinals.

At which point, reenter the Portinari brothers. Cosimo had taken the three boys, Pigello, Accerito, and Tommaso, into his home when their father, head of the Florence branch, died in 1431. At that point the eldest was ten, the same age as Giovanni di Cosimo, Piero's younger brother. But while the Medici boys got their expensive humanist education, reading Cicero and Caesar, Pigello Portinari left the Medici household at thirteen to start work in the bank—first in Rome, then in Venice—until in 1452 he was given the directorship of the newly opened branch in Milan, which immediately took on an aristocratic air. Francesco Sforza had given Cosimo various buildings in disrepair to house the bank. Cosimo brought in Michelozzo, who transformed them into a wonderful and very grand *palazzo*. Pigello Portinari thus spent his early years as director concerning himself to a large degree with interior decorating, importing tapestries, and commissioning artists. After all, much of the bank's capital was taken up in loans to the duke, loans repaid by allowing the bank to collect local taxes. So high was the interest rate on these loans that Pigello was able to attract capital from other Medici branches in order to keep funding the duke and his family's lavish expenditures. Milan thus soaked up considerable resources without producing any wealth. Everybody was living extravagantly on borrowed time. When that time began to run out, and even the duchy's tax revenues were not enough to repay the interest owed, the bank simply took back, as collateral, many of the jewels that the Sforzas had been persuaded to buy and sent them off to safes in Venice, in case the local authorities in Milan should ever decide to seize them.

This pointless tying-up of capital was hardly satisfactory, but at least Pigello was honest. In 1464, however, against all past practices of the bank, he was allowed to take on his brother Accerito as his deputy. It was the core of an entourage, the kind of thing Cosimo had always been careful to avoid. After Pigello died in 1468, Accerito was furious when Piero sent a mere employee from Florence to examine the branch's books. Accerito refused to show them. The bank had made all kinds of unwise loans and expenses. Francesco Sforza had died, leaving massive debts. "Accerito puffs up more and more every day," complained Francesco Nori, the would-be inspector. "My dear brother Pigello is already forgotten," wrote the third brother, Tommaso Portinari, from the bank in Bruges to Piero. "It's disgraceful your checking up on him." The veiled appeal to family connections did the job. Piero caved in and gave the directorship of Milan to Accerito, who proceeded to lose more and more money in interminable loans to the duke's family until the branch was finally closed in 1478.

MEANWHILE, OTHER FLORENTINE banks were going under altogether. In the mid-1420s, there had been seventy-two; in 1470, there were only thirty-three, with a half-dozen failures in the mid-1460s around the time Piero was calling in loans. The main reason for these failures, no doubt, was falling trade—a decline for which historians have yet to provide a complete explanation—and the bad debts of extravagant princes. Yet one can't help feeling that at a very deep level the whole Florentine attitude to banking had changed. The old humility, the old enthusiasm for the nitty-gritty of moneymaking, was gone. The families traditionally involved in banking were now used to their wealth and looking for other forms of excitement. Tommaso Portinari is emblematic.

If Cosimo's mind had reached out across Europe—planning, calculating, spinning his web across the continent's financial centers—his son Piero's poor head, when obliged to take his father's position at the center, was simply pained by the many tugs on that web. Piero, in the end, did no more than react to bad news. Most of it was coming from Tommaso Portinari in Bruges.

Having been part of the Medici household since he was three, Tommaso started work in the Bruges branch in 1445 at sixteen. This was shortly before the crisis brought about by the collapse of Venturi & Davanzati in Barcelona in 1447 and then the firing of his older cousin, Bernardo Portinari, who had set up the branch. The 1447 crisis, as we have seen, had to do with the bank's traditional business of interest-bearing exchange deals linked to triangular trading patterns. Brought up in the Palazzo Medici amid some of the city's finest artworks and in a constant back-and-forth of politicians, ambassadors, and heads of state, Tommaso set his sights instead on grander things. "Stop spending so much time at court," Piero was already writing to warn him when he was still a mere clerk. "Who could have spread such a vicious slander?" Tommaso replied. He was trying, he claimed, to secure a first sale of Florentine silk to the duke. "Will you give me an assistant?" he coolly adds. Piero wouldn't.

This was the duke of Burgundy, a principality that at that time occupied an area in the east of modern France stretching as far north as the English Channel, where it bordered with English territories around Calais, and then farther east up the Channel coast into modern Belgium. The dukes of Burgundy had occasionally been tempted to get involved in the Hundred Years' War, usually on the English side against their traditional rivals, the French. Tommaso, with no prompting or brief from the bank, had got himself made counselor to the young regent and later duke of Burgundy, Charles *le Téméraire,* usually translated in English as Charles the Bold, though the more accurate rendering would be Charles the Rash. A duke who had earned such a name might well need a counselor, but who would lend him money? Tommaso, of course, had been given the position of counselor precisely because he was able and willing to lend money. Not his own, but the Medici bank's. Just as Giovanni Tornabuoni in Rome had run down his boss, Leonardo Vernacci, in letters to the Medici family back in Florence, so Tommaso began to write nasty things about his director, Agnolo Tani. "A Turk!" he told Piero. "The customers hate him!"

Tani, like Vernacci, was of the old school, a cautious, crotchety, capable banking man with no particular family connections. "I will resign from the bank if he comes back," Tommaso threatened when Tani was away on a trip to Florence. This was 1465. Overwhelmed by other worries, Piero gave Tommaso what he wanted, the top position. After all, the two men had been brought up in the same home, presumably shared the same interests. At this point, the Rome, Milan, and Bruges branches of the bank were all being run by directors who felt they had special claims on the Medici family, special privileges, men who didn't like to think of themselves "merely" as bankers. In 1470, Lionetto di Benedetto d'Antonio de' Rossi was given the directorship of the once-prosperous branch in Geneva, which had now moved, together with Europe's main trade fairs, to Lyon in France. Lionetto had recently married Piero's illegitimate daughter, Maria, and thus was Lorenzo *il Magnifico*'s brother-in-law. Which makes four key branches in the hands of men who can't be fired.

No sooner is he director of the Bruges branch than Tommaso Portinari decides that the bank needs a *palazzo* comparable with the one his brother presides over in Milan. Hotel Bladelin, one of the finest buildings in Bruges, costs 7,000 Rhine florins. "And I do not live in pomp and show!" he protests in a letter to Piero. Impatient with ordinary banking trade, Tommaso goes remorselessly for the deal to end all deals. Giovanni Arnolfini—made famous by Jan van Eyck—has a concession to collect the customs duties on goods passing by cart or mule train from English-held Calais to the Low Countries. The collection point is the small coastal town of Gravelines. Counseling the duke, Tommaso takes over the contract for the Medici bank for 16,000 francs a year. Rash Charles has just banned the import of finished English wool cloth. Surely, Tommaso reasons, this will lead to a huge increase in raw wool imports, taxed at a higher rate. Can't lose. Instead, the English take reprisals. They want to work that wool themselves. They refuse to be pushed around like this. Trade falls drastically. By the summer of 1471, income from the Gravelines concession is close to zero.

The duke of Burgundy has built a couple of galleys for Pope Pius II's planned crusade against the ever-threatening Turk. The crusade is abandoned when Pius dies while waiting at the Adriatic seaside for his army to materialize. This in 1464. The duke now has two expensive galleys on his hands. Can counselor Tommaso sell them? With trade declining, there are no takers. To do *le Téméraire* a favor, the enterprising Tommaso buys the galleys for the Medici bank with Medici money. They can trade under the flag of the duke of Burgundy (the duke is flattered), thus evading Florentine taxes when they unload in Pisa. It's another white elephant. Come 1469, when it's time to renew Portinari's five-year contract, Piero, now in the last stages of terminal illness, introduces a special clause to the otherwise-standard branch director format:

> With the court of Burgundy or other lords or princes you must deal as little as possible . . . because the dangers are greater than the profits and many merchants have ended up badly in this way. . . . From this and other great enterprises you must steer clear, because our intention is to do business to conserve what we have of material goods, of credit and of honor, not to seek to get richer at great danger.

It's curious reading these words of solid commercial wisdom from a man who has just launched his son into the spendthrift elite of international blue blood and who himself has spent lavishly on political ends. A certain schizophrenia is at work. Piero has one foot in the old world, one in the new. He fords the stream. Not so the young Lorenzo, who, shortly after his father's death, will proudly confess to Agnolo Tani, still a major partner in the Bruges branch, that "I know nothing about such matters." Meaning banking.

Tommaso Portinari had ridden on horseback all the way from Bruges to Florence to sign that new contract. And to get married. Having returned to Bruges, he felt bound to apologize to Piero for having kept this second purpose of his visit secret. Why had he done that? Why not celebrate his wedding openly? For the simple reason that, with their growing power, the Medici had taken to arranging not only their own marriages but, as in the case of Giovanni Tornabuoni, everybody else's as well. Cosimo began it, Piero continued, and Lorenzo would excel in this department. While the Medici married up into the aristocracy, all the other noble families must marry down into the middle classes. A gap would be established. Society would thus be arranged around the Medici, for the Medici, and, most important, *beneath* the Medici. Tommaso, who grew up under their wing, was cutting free, as they had cut free from the Florentine mesh by having Lorenzo marry an Orsini. Piero was spared the pain of this wicked slight because he was dead when Portinari's letter of apology arrived.

Tommaso was now forty. His bride, Maria di Francesco di Bandini Baroncelli, was fifteen. The proud husband immediately had portraits painted by Hans Memling, with the well-bred adolescent wearing the pointed hat (with drapes) of the Flemish well-to-do, plus a lavish necklace of the kind the Officers of the Night would gladly have confiscated back in Florence. Is a pattern emerging: Tornabuoni, Sassetti, Portinari? After Tommaso and Maria's first children arrived, the whole family would appear kneeling in prayer on either side of Ugo van der Goes's bizarre and beautiful *Adoration of the Shepherds,* a painting that would cause such a stir when it arrived as an altarpiece in Florence. Meantime, despite that tough new clause in his contract, the loans to the duke of Burgundy continued and, come 1473, the Medici bank was still running those miserable, loss-making galleys when they were set upon by pirates off the Channel coast at Gravelines. The *San Giorgio* escaped. The *San Matteo* was captured, thirteen of its crew killed, and its cargo seized—another big loss for the bank—including a *Last Judgment* by Memling commissioned by Tommaso's ex-boss, Agnolo Tani. Instead of going to Florence, the painting ended up in Danzig, where it remains to this day.

WITH OR WITHOUT the "last judgment," the writing was definitely on the wall for the bank. In 1467, Tani had been sent to London to see if he could turn around the now-familiar scene of excessive lending to the local monarch—in this case, Edward IV. During the financial crisis of the mid-1460s, it had been imperative for Piero to guarantee a flow of raw wool to Florence—not just for his own workshops but also to maintain employment in general and prevent the kind of labor unrest that would feed opposition to the Medici regime. Again political convenience was bad news for the bank, since to get the export licenses for the raw wool from England, the London branch had had to do endless favors for the king. "I well understand, that what I have to do here," Tani wrote back to Piero once he had seen the accounts, "is resurrect the dead, no less." Did he already have Memling's commission in mind? "But if you and Tommaso do what I say, then with the grace of God. . . ."

Nobody did what he said. Giovanni Tornabuoni in Rome refused to accept finished English cloth in part-payment for the London branch's debt. Later, suddenly fearing he would never be paid at all, he lost his nerve, hurried to Florence, and seized a huge quantity of cloth that Tani had sent from London to pay monies owed to Bruges, and that Bruges had then sent on to Italy (in those famous Burgundy galleys) in part-payment of their debt toward the Florence branch. Tornabuoni's seizure of the cloth was illegal and the source of endless future accounting headaches; Francesco Sassetti as general director of the Medici bank should have prevented it, or at least censured it. But Tornabuoni was Lorenzo il Magnifico's uncle. He was family, whereas Agnolo Tani was just a conscientious bank manager. The London branch now owed the Rome branch more than 40,000 florins, and with Pope Paul II borrowing heavily, it was becoming more and more urgent for Tornabuoni—who, as a shareholding partner in the Rome venture was liable for eventual losses—to receive prompt payment of the papal tributes that the other branches were collecting.

In London, however, it was clear to Tani that his only chance of saving the branch lay in accepting as payment for loans the one product the English wanted to give him, finished wool cloth, and getting the other branches of the Medici bank to sell it all over Europe. "Please advance me 3,000 florins for the cloth you have received," he begged Sassetti in Florence. But Sassetti wouldn't pay anything until the cloth was sold. He sent letters of cautious advice. "We need help, not advice," Tani growled, this time writing directly to Lorenzo de' Medici. "A quarter of the men in this kingdom are lawyers so I get advice in plenty. . . . Before I came here everybody was telling me to perform miracles, but now you've all gone quiet."

In 1468, when King Edward's sister, Margaret, became the duke of Burgundy's third wife, Tani took advantage of the lavish celebrations to sell the king 6,000 florins' worth of Florentine silk. Quite a coup. But in order to get the sale, he had to make another loan. To have any clout when collecting loans, it seemed one must always appear to have more to lend. In the end, only the willingness of the Milan branch of the bank to advance London money against receipt of finished English cloth eventually allowed Tani to accomplish his mission and return the London branch, if not to health, then at least to some kind of zombie status. In the spring of 1469, the aging manager made the punishing trip back to Italy, on horseback, no doubt determined to tell the Medici that if the various branches of the bank were not better directed and coordinated, then before very long the whole network would collapse.

No sooner had Tani left England than the War of the Roses, which had brought Edward IV to the throne in 1461, broke out again. This time, in October 1470, Edward lost power and all the Medici money with it. The bank was again in desperate straits. Having fled to the Netherlands, however, Edward regrouped his forces and in May 1471 returned to England and won back his throne. But the Medici had no cause for celebration. Not only had Edward had to borrow heavily to pay for his military campaigns, making it even less likely that he would pay back the bank, but to make matters worse, a long roll call of other noble Medici debtors lay dead on the battlefields of Barnet and Tewkesbury, where Edward had triumphed.

Together with his appetite for the aristocratic life, Francesco Sassetti, at the head of the organization, was also afflicted by a chronic inability to fire anyone. The two character traits are united perhaps in the love of ease, comfort, cordial relations. In any event, when the efficient Tani left London, having just about turned around the bank's fortunes there, Sassetti did not take the opportunity to replace the local manager, Gherardo Canigiani, who had been largely responsible for causing the mess that Tani had gone to sort out. One would have thought that the crises of the previous years would have demonstrated once and for all the folly of tying up a bank's capital in loans to a monarch who not only was barely solvent but liable at any moment to be overwhelmed by civil war. So if, on Edward's return, Canigiani at once started extending fresh credit to the king, he presumably knew, as Portinari knew when he lent money to Charles the Bold, that he was not operating in the best interests of his employer. At last smelling a rat that was now in an advanced stage of decay, the Medici bank closed down its London operation in 1472 and terminated its contract with Canigiani, who promptly obtained a letter of naturalization from Edward IV, married a rich woman, and, with the king's help, became a very proper English country gentleman with lands in Buckinghamshire and his own coat of arms.

While men such as Agnolo Tani, Leonardo Vernacci, and Francesco Nori (the man who had tried to inspect Accerito Portinari's accounts in Milan) were serious and attentive bankers of the old Florentine school, ever anxious about the bottom line, others, it seemed, were only *playing* at banking in order to be close to kings and queens. Resurrecting the Medici business in this world was not of great importance to men like Canigiani and Tommaso Portinari, so long as they themselves could be reborn in the next: the world of royalty, art, and luxury clothing. As a major shareholder in Bruges, Tani was furious when he heard that, behind his back, Tommaso Portinari, in his role as director, had agreed that the branch would take on all London's debts when the English operation was wound up. Why on earth had Portinari done such a stupid thing? The only answer is: to be close to the London bank's major debtor, King Edward IV, now in military alliance with his rash Burgundy brother-in-law, planning the great invasion of France, which would eventually be launched in 1475.

THERE IS A moment, a written statement, in the history of the Medici that all the history books quote. On the evening after Piero's death, December 2, 1469, some seven hundred citizens met in the Convent of Sant'Antonio and agreed that the "reputation and greatness" of the Medici family must be preserved. "By which they mean," explained the ambassador of Ferrara to his lord, "that the secret things of this government will pass through Lorenzo's hands as before through his father's." The following day, a group of leading citizens went to the Palazzo Medici to give Lorenzo, who was about to turn twenty-one, the news. And we come to the famous quotation, from Lorenzo's brief *ricordi,* or memoirs:

> Though I, Lorenzo, was very young, being twenty years of age, the principal men of the city and of the regime came to us in our house to mourn our loss and to encourage me to take charge of the city and the regime as my grandfather and my father had done. The which being contrary to my age and involving great responsibilities and perils, I accepted with reluctance, and only to preserve our friends and possessions, for in Florence things can go badly for the rich if they don't run the state.

The history books then take sides. Fifteenth-century Florentine factionalism has proved a remarkably resilient disease. Five hundred years on, hardly a scholar escapes infection. So the detractors point out that only two days before Piero's death, Lorenzo had written to Galeazzo Sforza, duke of Milan, to ask for military help to guarantee his succession. This hardly looks like reluctance. The supporters, on the other hand, note that as an accomplished poet, Lorenzo did indeed have other interests. In the future, various poems would speak eloquently of the desire to abandon power and responsibility, which are seen as a prison rather than a privilege.

In the heat of this debate, the most intriguing aspect of the statement passes without comment: the words in the quotation sound as though written decades after the event from the vantage point of middle age and maturity; in fact, Lorenzo wrote them when he was only twenty-four. Still at the beginning of his rule, that is, he was already imagining how it would be seen later; he was inventing his persona, preparing material for the historians. "He behaves like an old man," remarked the ambassador to Milan approvingly in 1469 when Lorenzo was only twenty. But then, as Piero's son, the boy had been sent on his first diplomatic missions when still in his early teens. Power, together with a humanist education that concentrated on the great political leaders of antiquity, had created something Cosimo could not have foreseen: an extraordinary self-consciousness. Aware of his special situation, equipped with an abundance of role models, Lorenzo was playing a part. Not a real prince, he must *act* the prince. There were so many adults to impress.

"WITHOUT PLATONISM MAN can be neither a good citizen, nor a good Christian," Lorenzo de' Medici would one day claim. What on earth did he mean by that? And why, though his grandfather would never have made such a claim, did the old Cosimo become so interested in Plato in the last years of his life?

Greek philosophy was recovered and revived somewhat later than Roman. One simple reason was language. Greek was hardly taught until the middle of the fifteenth century. But even when Plato had been read, in Latin translation, by the great humanist (and Cosimo's friend) Leonardo Bruni, for example, the old Greek wasn't taken seriously. These self-regarding fantasies about philosopher kings, Bruni thought, were completely impractical. Plato's notions of a hierarchical stairway of realities, with inanimate material at the bottom and a world of ideal forms at the top, had already been widely appropriated and interminably elaborated by early Christian theologians in one form or another. It was theoretical nonsense. Stepping outside of medieval scholasticism and Christian mysticism for a breath of fresh air, the early humanists were looking for clear-sighted, secular wisdom, the lucidity of historians and political commentators: Cicero, Livy.

Under Cosimo's protection—a house and a salary—Marsilio Ficino translated the entire works of Plato into Latin in the 1460s. It was the first time they had all appeared in a form Western Christendom could read. Later to become a priest, Ficino added his own personal but crucial twist to Christian Platonism: The human soul, he decided, was "the center of nature," the connecting link between the hierarchies of Platonic reality. Through love and intellect, the human soul *naturally* strives upward, away from what is base and earthly, through the hierarchy, to the pure light of perfect eternity, God.

Discussed by Florence's best minds, while celebrating Plato's birthday, for example, every November 7 at the Medici villa at Careggi, such ideas came at exactly the right moment for the process of upward social transformation in which the Medici were involved. Apart from giving a new sense to courtly love poetry (the mind moving from profane to divine love), all education, refinement, and intellectual achievement could now be understood as essentially moral, involved in a process of striving toward the Divine. Certain secular activities, that is, could be described as partaking of the sacred, or at least as turned *toward* the sacred. Nothing good (and the dangerous implication is that we know instinctively what is good) was outside the Christian framework. At which point art and poetry need no longer turn so constantly to strictly Christian subject matter, because beauty itself is close to divinity and the human soul naturally leans toward it. Creativity, which is of God, is not, in this new and optimistic version of Platonism, denied to man, though few achieve it. But when achieved, it is essentially good. Even today, there are many who believe that art is necessarily *on the right side,* and do not ask which bank sponsored it. Sponsored by Medici money, Botticelli can use the same pretty model for a Madonna, or for Venus. He can leave the lady's clothes on or he can lift them off. Either way, the mind is being lifted spiritually. At this point, the gesture of penance implicit in almost all Cosimo's patronage of the arts can be safely and happily forgotten. Art is always sacred.

But to dig a little deeper, at what wasn't explicitly stated or perhaps even consciously meant, yet nevertheless seeps through: the process of raising yourself up, of becoming this refined, educated, artistic aristocrat, was now no longer an evil thrusting above and beyond your proper medieval station (as the treason charge against Cosimo in 1433 implied). On the contrary, it was a sign of your upward aspiration toward the Divine. This was an attractive and soothing thought. It would galvanize Lorenzo into sponsoring, and himself engaging in, a range of lavish, public artistic projects, mainly secular, which were at once beautiful and politically convenient, in that they enhanced his and the city's image. A leader who sponsors and, as a poet, actually creates beautiful art cannot be a bad leader. A leader who employs the likes of Botticelli to make festival banners and carnival floats will not get a bad press from posterity. And the good citizen, the good Christian, must be a Platonist because only the Platonist appreciates and participates in this striving for the beautiful and better, this aestheticizing of public life. If he wasn't a Platonist, that is, our philistine citizen might merely start counting the florins and *piccioli* and making dry remarks about political self-interest.

Which brings us to the chief drawback of these exciting ideas: They had little to say about moneymaking and the price of things. The underlying contradiction here is quite different from Cosimo's dilemma: How do I get my soul to heaven while amassing a fortune with supposedly sinful banking practices. The problem now is that while wealth is actually more important than ever—for how else can you get the best artists, the best teachers, a decent translation of Plato, not to mention the wherewithal to throw a lavish party for a dead philosopher's birthday?—nevertheless the actual process of moneymaking is passed over as something base, something on the lowest level of the Platonic hierarchy, something the nobler soul would gladly leave behind in its struggle to be free from mere matter.

To this frame of mind, then, the complexities of accountancy, the intricate technicalities by which the sin of usury can be avoided, are no longer things to dwell on with pleasure, as Cosimo doubtless did dwell on them—Cosimo who said he would be a banker even if money could be made by waving a wand. No, now the cultured man wants to wave whatever wand comes to hand and get the problem of a good income *out of the way* as soon as possible: by lending money to the duke of Milan at the highest possible rate of interest, for example; by getting the concession to collect import duties at the customs post of Gravelines; or, most dramatically, in the case of the Medici bank, by the attempt to establish a permanent gold mine with the alum affair.

What was the alum affair? "It makes me think of the Holy Spirit," wrote Gentile Becchi, Lorenzo's tutor. "I don't understand it." Ironically, the two extremes of Christian Platonism's hierarchy of realities—base matter, divine essence—seem to have become equally incomprehensible to the educated mind located somewhere in between. In any event, the eagerness to have the money problem *out of the way* thanks to this base material, alum—an aluminum sulfate used, among other things, for dyeing cloth—would plunge Lorenzo into the great defining dramas of his life, where the part he was learning to play would demand a divine performance.

6

The Magnificent Decline

First son after three sisters, his mere arrival was a triumph. Vast resources stooped over him, anxious to be of use. Even his wet nurse received begging letters.

Spectacularly ugly, he was brought up to seduce. At the age of five, he was dressed as a little French boy to greet Prince Jean d'Anjou. Alas, his nose was flattened on his face. At the age of ten, he recited poems for the visiting Galeazzo Maria Sforza, for Pope Pius II. His protruding jaw pushed the lower lip above the upper. He learned to play the viola and the lute. He learned to ride on horseback and to hold the falcon. Deprived of any sense of smell, he began to write poetry full of flowers and bees. It was love poetry. At the age of sixteen, his bumpy forehead and bushy eyebrows had won the heart of pretty Lucrezia Donati. Hoarse and unpleasantly high-pitched to the ear, in verse his voice chimed with precocious harmony. "Tender age will not forego to follow Love." He knew his models: Petrarch, Dante, Ovid. With charming assurance, he elaborated his pain. "So cruel the first wound was!" Young Lucrezia was promised to someone else.

Already men wrote to him begging favors: stonecutters, farmers, painters, poets. And Lorenzo interceded with his father on their behalf: I trust you will "honor me in this," the Medici heir solemnly writes, when gouty Piero is no more than a couple of rooms away. Other people's anxieties prompt exercises in style. Surrounded by some of the finest minds of the time, the young man discussed the consolations of philosophy, the nature of good government. "He stays out late," complained his tutor in a letter to the boy's parents, "flirting with the girls and playing pranks."

Formal visits to other courts began when he was in his early teens. Aware of that ugly face, that grating voice, he dazzled with an extraordinary intellectual energy. In Milan, he threw parties in the bank's magnificent premises and met Ippolita Sforza, the duke's daughter, who was about to marry the son of the king of Naples. The two adolescents exchanged letters, on literary matters, and later Ippolita asked for a loan of 2,000 ducats. "I promise on my honor I will pay it back."

In 1466, now seventeen, he was sent down to Rome to sign some dull contract regarding the merchandising of alum, a mineral essential to the wool trade. It is his first involvement in banking business. Fortunately, the death of Francesco Sforza turns the trip into a dramatic diplomatic mission. He must convince the pope that the duke's son should be allowed to succeed as lord of Milan. Sforza had been a usurper. Sforza is the Medici's main ally. Lorenzo must hurry down to Naples to check that King Ferrante has no alternative arrangements in mind.

Returning to Florence in time for his father's showdown with

Lorenzo de' Medici, in a bust attributed to Verrocchio. Hardly Adonis, Lorenzo was obliged to master other forms of seduction. He remains one of the finest of fifteenth-century poets.

the anti-Medici conspirators—Pitti, Acciaiuoli, Dietisalvi, and Soderini—Lorenzo makes his dramatic appearance together with the troops from Milan, armed and on horseback, at the parliament in the Piazza della Signoria. It is a gesture at once of seduction and coercion. Florence must love me. An artistic gesture. The young man dismounts and stands together, as an equal, with the priors in their red robes as the request for a *balia* with unlimited powers is read out, and the people, surrounded by armed men, vote away their republican rights. It is in the nature of every artist to combine seduction and coercion. The public must succumb to my point of view, to the point of my sword. There is no radical split between Lorenzo the poet and Lorenzo the politician. Way below the eligible age for public service, he was nevertheless given a place on the *balia,* which, with its unlimited powers, would once again put the city firmly in Medici hands.

Alum, one suspects, was not on Lorenzo's mind as he faced the Florentine people in the piazza at that moment of crisis. But it was present everywhere. It was with alum that raw wool from England was cleansed of its grease. Everyone in the square was wearing wool. It was alum that fixed the dyes in the priors' crimson gowns and alum that cured the leather on the horsemen's saddles. And three years later, in 1469, when Lorenzo married Clarice Orsini by proxy and, in her absence, celebrated this great step from merchant to aristocrat with a lavish tournament in Piazza Santa Croce, alum was present again in another way. This gritty white sulfate was largely responsible for paying the 10,000 or more florins that the event is reputed to have cost.

Pearls and velvet abounded at that expensive celebration.

Young Lorenzo carried a standard given to him not by his new wife but by his old girlfriend, Lucrezia Donati. It showed a woman twining a laurel crown, for her poet. And since Lucrezia was queen of the tournament, it was she, and not Lorenzo's new but absent wife, who placed a silver helmet on the warrior's head when, inevitably, the family who had financed the event had its boy win. What Lorenzo had signed down in Rome in 1466 was a contract giving the Medici the total monopoly over all sales of alum throughout Christendom. There is no indication from his writings that Lorenzo had grasped the importance of this. Perhaps what mattered more was that Lucrezia too was married now, though her husband was abroad on business. People were gossiping. Meanwhile, Clarice, married and virgin, wrote from Rome to say that the mere thought of Lorenzo's being involved in a tournament had given her a migraine. From a family of real soldiers, and with no experience of Florence and its amorous ways, she could be forgiven for mistaking the real source of danger. "All libidinous and venereal," as Guicciardini described him, "marvelously involved in things of Venus," as Machiavelli added, Lorenzo continued to write poetry. To Lucrezia.

MONOPOLIES, LIKE USURY, were illegal under Church law. Because unnatural. God had given the natural world to all mankind, not to a chosen few. Denying people liberty and keeping prices artificially high, monopolies were obviously a form of stealing and could only lead to perdition. As with usury, the Church insisted that only full restitution of ill-gotten gains could make amends and get you to heaven, though it is difficult to see how, after exercising a monopoly for some years, you could ever calculate the exact amount of what had been stolen, or from whom.

The Church's concept of the monopoly was not restricted to the situation where a single organization had control over the sale of a particular product. To form a workers' union, for example, was also a monopoly, and of the most pernicious variety: It restricted freedom of labor and the right of an employer to hire any worker on any terms. A union was *unnatural*. Any association of woolworkers, for example, in this cloth-manufacturing town of Florence, was immediately condemned and crushed.

Despite this exemplary strictness, in 1466 Pope Paul II declared that the Church, in alliance with the Medici bank, would now operate a monopoly on the sale of alum throughout Europe. After salt and iron, alum was the most important mineral of the time. Without it, the cloth trade could hardly have functioned. But how could the Church justify such a flagrant breach of its own laws? The profits from this ambitious commercial venture, said the Holy Father, would go toward a new crusade against the Turks. This made the monopoly not only legal but virtuous. It was a case of the desirable end justifying the otherwise-sinful means. A dangerous precedent for a religious organization.

Here are the circumstances. The annual European market for alum was worth something in excess of 300,000 florins, almost ten times what the king of England owed the Medici bank. Only a very small amount of the mineral was actually mined in Christendom, on the island of Ischia at the northwest entrance to the Bay of Naples. The quality of this deposit was poor, so poor that in some northern European markets its use was banned, because potentially harmful to the wool it was supposed to treat. Hence most alum had to come from mines in the Gulf of Izmir, on the eastern shores of the Aegean, now under the control of the Turks, and hence Islam. These mines had been developed for the most part by the Genoese, who thus controlled most of the trade in alum, paying taxes and customs duties to the Turks and thus helping to finance the constant Turkish expansion into Christendom, through Eastern Europe.

In 1460, the Italian merchant Giovanni da Castro, whose father had been a close friend of Pope Pius and who had recently escaped from creditors in the Eastern Mediterranean to live under the pontiff's protection in Rome, discovered a huge deposit of high-quality alum in the mountains of Tolfa, northeast of Rome. Understanding the importance of the discovery, Pius at once declared this barren area of land to be Church property. Castro would mine and refine the alum and the Church would market it, thus gaining a huge income for themselves and taking away a huge income from their enemies, the Turks.

To market the mineral on a wide scale, however, both credit and commercial expertise were necessary. Hence in 1466, Pius's successor, Paul II, decided to make a contract with the Medici bank that allowed them to use their Europe-wide trade network to sell whatever the Italian mine produced. At the same time, Pope Paul announced that any merchant found to be purchasing Turkish alum would be punished with excommunication, since buying from the Turks what could be bought from the pope amounted to aiding the attack on Christendom. All this came as very bad news for the Venetians, who had recently taken over from the Genoese the concession to work the alum mines in the Gulf of Izmir.

In 1470 the papal monopoly was firmed up by establishing an alum producers' cartel with the owners of the mine in Ischia and with the king of Naples, to whom those owners paid a duty on whatever they produced. Under this agreement, the entire volume of alum mined and refined for the European market would be controlled by the Church in such a way as to keep the prices as high as possible, a sort of fifteenth-century OPEC. Only a year after signing up to the cartel, however, the Medici and Pope Paul pulled out when it became clear that Ischia would never be a dangerous competitor, and this for the simple reason that wool manufacturers much preferred the better-quality alum from Tolfa.

At first glance, such a coup seems to put the Medici bank in a league of its own. They now have sole rights to sell one of the most important industrial products of their time. Those rights are backed up by the threat of excommunication. In Rome, Giovanni Tornabuoni is absolutely convinced that all the bank's problems are now solved. This is the dream deal that everybody has been looking for, the deal that will take all the tedium and risk out of banking and allow important people like himself and Tommaso Portinari to spend more of their time building up their libraries, commissioning paintings, attending lavish functions at court, and, in general, behaving more like their Medici masters.

Alas, it was not to be. In England, in Burgundy, in Venice—the main markets for alum—monarchs and merchants were not as impressed as they had once been by the threat of excommunication. It was hard to feel that what you had been doing in good conscience all your life had suddenly become a mortal sin. They employed local theologians to argue the case against the papal monopoly. A sin (like a monopoly) is always a sin, these wise men decided, even if the profits from it, at least as far as the pope was concerned, were indeed being used to pay the Hungarian king to fight the Turks. In Bruges, Tommaso Portinari counseled and counseled rash Duke Charles of Burgundy, begging him to impose the alum monopoly throughout his dukedom and ban sales of the mineral from any source other than the Medici bank. Offered a cut on profits, the duke at first agreed. But however rash he might have been, Charles recognized the signs of rebellion when he saw them. The local merchants, both importers and end users, were furious. The wool trade was at risk, they said. In the end, the duke backed down. Turkish alum continued to arrive in the port of Bruges.

When planning production at the mines in Tolfa and Ischia, the monopolists had imagined they would have the market entirely to themselves. They aimed to meet the entire European demand in just a few years. So when the threat of excommunication failed to stop the Venetians and Genoese from dealing in Turkish alum, the sudden glut caused by supplies from both sources made it hard to maintain old prices, let alone increase them as the monopolists had planned. Bulk buyers of alum in London and Bruges formed associations and lobbies to increase their negotiating power. The papal percentage on incomes from sales had to be halved, which soon meant less money to fund the Hungarian king.

To make matters worse—at least as far as the Medici bank was concerned—this venture into merchandising alum represented another blow to the already-precarious balance of trade and movement of money among the bank's various branches. Here was yet another product moving north from Italy. Once again cash would have to be collected in London and Bruges and sent south. Why couldn't the alum have been discovered in the Cotswolds, for heaven's sake, to replace the wool the English were now so reluctant to sell? That would have been so convenient. Unwisely, in return for its rights of monopoly, the bank had agreed to pay the pope his cut on whatever was mined *before* the product was shipped and sold.

Given the tensions between the Bruges and Rome branches of the bank, particularly since Giovanni Benci's death in 1455, the problems arising from the alum monopoly were predictable enough. As always, Bruges and London were slow to send money down to Rome. As always, Tornabuoni, in Rome, was impatient, suspecting as he did that Bruges and London were squandering the incomes from alum sales in loans to dukes and duchesses. An employee from the Rome branch was sent north to see what was going on. Then the pope sent his own negotiators to tackle the duke. But if there was one thing Tommaso Portinari loathed, it was interference. Papal spies! he complained in a letter to Lorenzo de' Medici. If I can't counsel the duke, what chance has a bishop got?

As the years pass, the situation deteriorates. A Florentine galley sinks. The cargo is lost. Then two galleys arrive simultaneously from Genoa and Venice, bringing Turkish alum. At this point, the port of Bruges is warehousing a three-year supply of the mineral all at once. Needless to say, the price collapses. More and more, the alum deal comes to assume the function of a chimera; if only the bank could really impose this monopoly, everything would be okay. But in the meantime, there are shipping costs and warehousing expenses and very little income. On March 18, 1475, Tornabuoni tells Lorenzo de' Medici that between paying the producers and the papal dues and the galleys, the bank is actually losing money on alum. Meantime, there was the Volterra affair.

ALONG WITH THE family's source of wealth, another thing to be *got out of the way,* in young Lorenzo's Neoplatonic vision of things, was the regime's hold on power. It seemed that whatever *balia,* council, or institution the Medici set up to guarantee their authority, as time passed even the most carefully selected allies began to vote along more republican lines. People have a stubborn bias toward freedom. When Lorenzo took over from his father, the *signoria* was being selected by nine *accoppiatori,* who in turn were selected annually by the Council of 100, the sort of permanent Medici *balia* established after the 1458 parliament. But the council was no longer doing as it was told. Lorenzo found he had to attend its assemblies in person if members weren't to vote against him. It was irritating. "I plan to behave the way my grandfather did," he had told the Milanese ambassador soon after his father's death, "which was to do these things in as civil a way as one can, and as far as possible within the constitution."

But how civil and constitutional can one be if one wants to have a rock-solid guarantee of remaining in power? Almost immediately, Lorenzo went far beyond his grandfather. By the end of 1471, the *signoria* was still being chosen by nine *accoppiatori,* but now the *accoppiatori* were chosen every July by their nine outgoing predecessors together with the *signoria* in office at the moment. Power was thus entirely circular. To console the Council of 100 for their loss of influence over the *accoppiatori* and hence the government, they were now allowed to ratify the decisions of the *signoria* directly, without the need of further ratification from the traditional Councils of the Commune and of the People—which more or less ceased to have any reason to exist.

At this point, the Medici are exercising almost complete control over the affairs of state. And yet a certain façade of constitutionality is maintained: The councils do meet and vote; the selection of the *signoria* is still recorded as though it were a fair lottery. Such pretenses of constitutionality quickly fell away when both banking income and political authority were threatened by the discovery of alum in Volterra.

Volterra is a small town some twenty miles southwest of Florence. In the fifteenth century, it was a subject community, paying a tribute to Florence but running its own government. Naturally, everybody was excited about the alum, then disappointed when the mining concession was given to a private consortium with Florentine backing. It was important, of course, for the Medici bank to bring this new source of the product into their monopoly. The government in Volterra, run by a faction opposed to the consortium, confiscated the mine. Florence intervened to reverse the decision.

This is June 1471. Lorenzo has had a busy eighteen months since his father died. A rebellion, instigated by the conspirators of

1466, was put down in Prato. There were executions. His first child, Lucrezia, was born in 1470 and his first son and heir, Piero, arrived in February 1471. Clarice was playing her part. In March, Lorenzo was host to Galeazzo Sforza, duke of Milan, who brought an embarrassingly large entourage and indulged the scandalous habit of eating meat during Lent. Inevitably, God showed his wrath by having the Church of Santo Spirito burn down, and the frightened Florentines did penance with some strict new laws on luxury clothes and foods.

Throughout his wife's pregnancies, Lorenzo continued to write love sonnets to Lucrezia Donati and was simultaneously working on a parodic *Symposium* of more than eight hundred lines featuring a wildly drunken evening among local philosophers and clergymen. It is hilarious. Certainly more of his time was given to this first experiment in satire than to the reopening of Medici bank branches in Venice and Naples.

Then, just as the Volterra crisis was hotting up, Pope Paul II died—this in July 1471—and Lorenzo had to hurry down to Rome for the coronation of Pope Sixtus IV. One can imagine how hard it was for a twenty-two-year-old to concentrate on politics, banking, babies, and poetry all at once. In his brief *ricordi,* Lorenzo describes the trip to Rome thus: "I was much honored, and brought back two antique marble busts of Augustus and Agrippa, that Pope Sixtus gave me, plus an inlaid cup of chalcedony and many other cameos and medals that I purchased." Though he wrote these memories in 1473, Lorenzo doesn't mention the most important event of his rule to date, the sacking of Volterra. It was not something to be proud of.

With the quarrel between the mining consortium and the town's ruling faction deadlocked, the Volterrans appeal to Lorenzo to arbitrate. Predictably enough, Lorenzo decides that the alum consortium, which includes two prominent, pro-Medici Volterrans, should keep its concession. The opposing faction rebels, riots, kills the two prominent Lorenzo supporters, and declares independence from Florence. Nevertheless, the aging counselor Tommaso Soderini tells Lorenzo that there really is no need to send an army. A crisis like this can be solved with patience and negotiation.

Soderini, who had remained faithful to the Medici throughout his elder brother's rebellion in 1466, was now pushing seventy. He was married to Lucrezia Tornabuoni's sister, Lorenzo's aunt, and, as the regime's most senior man, he no doubt expected to exercise a certain influence over his young nephew. But this was precisely the kind of presumption that Lorenzo would not accept. Less like his grandfather Cosimo than he claimed, Lorenzo was determined not just to be in charge, but to be *seen* to be so. He, a Medici, a man married into the Orsini family, a man who had hosted the duke of Milan in his *palazzo,* had been insulted, his friends killed.

Lorenzo hires and sends an army. After a month's siege, the Volterrans surrender on the understanding that their lives and properties will be spared. Entering the town, the mercenaries sack, rape, and kill. It is the right of a mercenary army to sack the town they have taken. Everybody knows that. From now on, the Volterrans will be Lorenzo's implacable enemies. Appalled by the bloodshed resulting from his decisions, Lorenzo tries to make amends with a personal gift to the Volterrans of 2,000 florins. It is less than a fifth of what had been spent on his famous marriage tournament three years earlier. Even before the material damage to the town can be repaired, the recently discovered alum mine is closed down. The deposit turns out to be scanty and the quality poor. The whole brutal affair has been completely unnecessary.

"LORENZO'S GREATEST FAILING," wrote the historian Guicciardini in 1509, "was suspicion." First of a new species—the aristocrat by education, marriage and money, rather than hereditary right—Lorenzo was afraid that others wouldn't recognize his superiority, then afraid, when they did, that they would try to bring him down. A pattern of behavior emerged: imagining himself threatened, or offended (it was the same thing), he would overreact and bring about the clash he feared. That was how the massacre in Volterra was provoked. There was worse to come.

Pope Sixtus, who had been so generous to Lorenzo with the chalcedony cups at his coronation, who supported him over the Volterra affair and even granted him and his mother and brother a plenary indulgence—a place in heaven no less—now tries to regain control of Città di Castello in the northern Papal States, not far from the southern borders of the Florentine Republic. The *signore* of the town—or usurper, as Sixtus sees it—is a friend of Lorenzo's and appeals for his help. Lorenzo immediately takes the pope's campaign as a personal affront and sends troops to help his friend, though not enough troops to do anything more than alienate the pope, his bank's most important client. Despite all the diplomatic missions in adolescence, Lorenzo is still a very young man to be running a state.

Pope Sixtus announces that he wants to buy the lordship of

Imola, a town northeast of Florence, for his nephew, Girolamo Riario. Almost everything Sixtus does, he does for his nephews. To secure the deal, however, he needs to borrow more than 40,000 florins. From his banker, obviously, who else? But Lorenzo feels that Imola should be in Florence's sphere of influence, not the pope's. Looking at the map, one can't help but agree. He refuses the money. He warns another Florentine bank dealing with the pope to refuse too. The Pazzi are an ancient and highly respected family—one old uncle and a dozen adult nephews—with an international bank similar in structure to that of the Medici. Not only do they go ahead and lend the cash to Sixtus, but they actually inform him of Lorenzo's attempt to stop them, as if the Medici were the merest commercial competitors and not the rulers of Florence. This is a major insult, and a big risk for the Pazzi. Clearly they feel that Lorenzo hasn't been giving their family the honors it deserves—for example, in the scrutiny of 1472 when the Pazzi got very few name tags in the electoral bags. Well, they certainly wouldn't be getting any more now.

In 1474, Pope Sixtus proposes Francesco Salviati as archbishop of Florence. But Salviati is a close friend of the Pazzi. The pope, however, despite Lorenzo's attempt to stop him from buying Imola, proves amenable to protest and nominates Lorenzo's brother-in-law, Rinaldo Orsini, instead. Which was generous. Then the archbishopric of Pisa falls vacant, and this time the pope appoints Salviati without consulting Lorenzo. In the meantime, he has ordered an audit on the Curia's alum accounts with the Medici bank. The price in Bruges and London has plummeted. The forecast income isn't forthcoming. Lorenzo is deeply offended. It's a dishonor to audit me! My family has served the pope for decades. And he denies the new archbishop, Salviati, right of entry to Pisa. Pisa is subject to Florence. I should have been consulted. No one can be bishop in Pisa without my consent. The pope threatens Lorenzo with excommunication. And he appoints a Pazzi as bishop down in Sarno near Naples.

"Puffed up by his Majesty [King Ferrante of Naples] . . . these Pazzi relatives of mine are seeking to harm me as much as they can." Thus Lorenzo in a letter to Duke Galeazzo Sforza in Milan, begging him to put pressure on the pope to withdraw the appointment of Salviati to the archbishopric of Pisa. Lorenzo refers to the Pazzi as relatives because his older sister Bianca has long been married to one of the Pazzi nephews, Guglielmo.

But Pisa is a battle Lorenzo can't win. The Church is too strong. Not long after Salviati is finally allowed to enter the town and take up his archbishopric, the pope declines to renew the Medici's alum monopoly and gives it instead to the Pazzi. Again the bank pays the consequences for the politicking that its wealth has made possible.

Would the tit-for-tat never end? Apparently not. In March 1477, a dispute arose between Giovanni Pazzi, another of the dozen nephews, and the cousin of his wife, Beatrice Borromei. The Borromei family was extremely rich. Beatrice's father had just died. Since Beatrice had no brothers or sisters, she expected to inherit the old man's wealth, which would thus enter into the Pazzi family. But her cousin, Carlo, disagreed. He seized part of the fortune and insisted that, being male, he should have it. Lorenzo intervened—Don't do this! his younger brother, Giuliano, warned him—to get a law passed that would give nephews precedence over daughters. This was a major change in social custom, no doubt affecting hundreds of lives, calculations, prospects. Despite urgent advice to the contrary, Lorenzo went ahead and the money was kept from the Pazzi family. "Giuliano de' Medici complained over and over to his brother," writes Machiavelli, "that by wanting too many things, all of them might be lost." As far as Giuliano was concerned, they were. He was assassinated by the Pazzi during mass in the *duomo* in April 1478. Lorenzo escaped.

THE HUMANISM OF the fifteenth century has generally received an enthusiastic press: the enquiring mind turns away from abstruse metaphysics to concentrate on what is human. That must be a good thing. Yet the phenomenon was so various, the *human* is so various, that it is truly hard to approve of every manifestation of the movement. Unless perhaps what most attracts us to humanism, what makes most of us humanists in fact, is the movement's greatest outrage: its dismissal of what came before as a thousand years of darkness, as if the middle ages had somehow been *inhuman*. Why did the humanists have to do that? Why is the dismissal still so important to us?

Marsilio Ficino, protégé of Cosimo de' Medici, spoke little of darkness but a great deal about illumination. Sixteen years older than Lorenzo, he made, in the early 1470s, a rather more successful bid than the aging patrician Soderini to influence the young ruler, presenting himself as a philosophical father to a privileged disciple, not an interested party with advice to give on contentious issues. As a thinker, Ficino's most characteristic gesture was conflation. Reading and translating widely, searching back in time long before Rome and abroad far east of the Aegean, he had an uncanny ability to find the same thing wherever he looked and above all to superimpose one tradition on another. The mountain Dante ascends in the *Commedia* is obviously the Olympus of the Greeks, the Pradesha or "supreme field" of Sanskrit, the Pardes of the Chaldeans, the Arab mountain of Qaf, and even the *mons Veneris* of sensual delight. The Orphic *Hymn to the Sun,* which Ficino translated, was clearly akin to Plato's metaphor of the cave and the light in *The Republic,* which Ficino translated, to the late classical theologian Proclus's *Hymn to the Sun,* which Ficino translated, and to St. Augustine's notion of God as "the sun of the soul," which, in the *Soliloquia,* Ficino both translated and wrote a commentary on. The whole world, it seemed, had always followed a single faith whose ancient priests included Zoroaster, Hermes Trismegistus, Orpheus, Pythagoras, Plato, St. Paul, St. Augustine.

Supremely eclectic, Ficino's humanism annihilated all divisions—this in stark contrast to the Christianity of the previous centuries, which had followed a single tradition, concentrated on an established canon of authors, yet managed to divide the world very sharply, perhaps depressingly, into good and bad, true and false, right and wrong, heaven and hell. This was why, for the humanists, the recent past had to be not so much argued with as surpassed, forgotten. It would not permit the thrill of the exotic, or a more personal selection of what to read and think. From now on instead, any argument would take place within a new *zona franca* where ancient met modern, East met West, and the excited mind was free to try out what it liked. Humanism, in short, unlocked the door to that supermarket of ideas we live in today.

There were aspects of Ficino's thought that were extremely attractive to Lorenzo. One of his conflations was the fairly common one of the authoritative father figure with the prince or political leader. Following the birth of his daughter Maddalena in 1473, Lorenzo was now a father three times over. *Father* is a more positive word than *tyrant*. Never one to leave anything out of an equation, Ficino brought in God and artists too, as analogous to fathers and princes: "The son is the work of the father, and there is nothing that man loves more than his own work. And this is why God loves human nature and authors their books, and painters the people they have painted." By the same mental process, Lorenzo would eventually be able to think of Florence as becoming—through his government, his marriage-arranging, his manipulation of available patronage to painters, poets, sculptors, and architects—his own personal work of art. He loved it because he was making it what it was. At which point, whether money flowed out of Lorenzo's purse toward the town or, more likely, with the bank's now-rapid decline, out of state coffers and into the Palazzo Medici, was unimportant. Father and son keep their money in common.

Nor was Ficino's eclecticism alien to elitism. The world had always been as he described it—the soul of man yearning for the divine light—yet it was not given to everybody to understand that. Most people would remain in ignorance. And this was how it should be. Ficino translated into Latin, after all, not into the vernacular. Only the best educated could read Latin. "Religious mysteries," wrote Pico della Mirandola, another disciple of Ficino's, "would not be mysteries if they did not remain occult." A fair point. The deeper truths could thus only be written about "under enigmatic veilings and poetic dissimulations." This explained the complex, often ambiguous nature of myth, and indeed many of the somewhat puzzling paintings of nymphs and satyrs that were beginning to flow from Sandro Botticelli's workshop. Only those already in the know, those who could afford to commission a painting, were to understand.

Certainly, after drawing close to Ficino, Lorenzo's sonnets to Lucrezia had changed. They became densely enigmatic. Old and obvious sensual urges (once they had been called sins) must now be conflated with mysticism's ancient ecstasies and the yearning for truth and beauty. This wasn't always easy. And as Lorenzo's rule over Florence progressed, the habit of political secrecy intensified too; "the secret things" grew more secret. The regime's leaders, it seems, had begun to think of themselves as initiates in a cult, of philosopher kings perhaps. A cult of power.

The longer Lorenzo ruled Florence, the less documentation we have of the deliberations of the various government committees. Only a few fragments of the bank's accounts remain from this period. What we do have instead, in refreshing contrast to the by-now-arcane love sonnets, are all the bawdy songs Lorenzo composed for the town's popular Carnival celebrations. Here the only conflation, as interminable as it is scabrous, was that of the *double entendre*. "Oh pretty women," ends his "Song of the Bakers," "such is our art: if you'd like something to pop in your mouths, try this for a start." The working men of the town must have loved it. Quite probably the women, too. One of the tenets of Ficino's Platonism was that you draw other souls to your position through song, as Orpheus drew Eurydice from the darkness with his lyre. You don't try to convince with reasoned argument. Here is Lorenzo's "Song of the Peasants":

Cucumbers we've got, and big ones,
Though to look at bumpy and odd
You might almost think they had spots on
But they open passages blocked
Use both hands to pluck 'em
Peel the skin from off the top
Mouths wide open and suck 'em
Soon you won't want to stop.

Ascending the Platonic categories of the spirit in his esoteric love sonnets, Lorenzo seduced his less-educated Florentine subjects with rhyming obscenities. Everyone agreed he was a genius. Who, one wonders, was using Cosimo's prayer cell in San Marco?

LORENZO HAS LEFT his infantile "games"—meaning his profane poems—to concentrate on "the Supreme Good." Thus Ficino, rather optimistically, in a letter to a friend in 1474. Lorenzo had now started a long and solemn work called *The Supreme Good,* which paraphrased Ficino's views. At the same time, the argument with the pope over the appointment of

Francesco Salviati had begun. Ficino was a good friend of Salviati's. This was embarrassing. And though the would-be archbishop was no Platonist, the Church as a whole was not hostile to the new humanist eclecticism. At one party thrown by Cardinal Pietro Riario—another friend of Salviati's and another of the nephews whom Pope Sixtus had elevated to high office—a poem was read out about how the gods of Olympus had refused to answer Jupiter's summons because they were busy serving the cardinal and his guests with, among other things, cakes designed to represent scenes from classical mythology. It's curious how this vertiginous mixing of traditions and upsetting of hierarchies (a god serving a cardinal!) always seemed to go hand in hand with the feeling that all the traditional codes of behavior could be broken. No pope had ever appointed so many members of his family to positions of power, whether spiritual or secular, as did Sixtus. Later, knowing full well that the plan was to kill Lorenzo and his brother Giuliano, the Holy Father would nevertheless give his blessing to the Pazzi conspiracy to oust the Medici, "so long as death doesn't come into it."

But the codes you broke depended on who you were and which of the classics you were reading. While Lorenzo and Ficino and friends were spending pleasant afternoons in Medici country villas playing Socrates and Alcibiades, while Giovanni Tornabuoni and Tommaso Portinari were having their images superimposed on various biblical scenes, a young man called Girolamo Logiati was reading Sallust's account of the conspiracy of Catiline in 63 B.C. In December 1476, imitating antique role models, Logiati and two fellow conspirators assassinated Galeazzo Maria Sforza, duke of Milan, at high mass on St. Stephen's Day. Perhaps one becomes aware that one has entered the modern world when even the most courageous of actions seem wrapped in a sticky film of parody, of inappropriate repetition. Sforza was a loathsome man, he had raped and tortured. But this was not republican Rome. The common people had not been reading Sallust. They did not rise up to celebrate their freedom. Instead they went after the conspirators. All three were executed.

When the grand virtues risk appearing as charade, or as borrowed from a different drama, the one sure value that remains is money. You can count it. You can weigh it. You can check it with your teeth. In Rome, Francesco Pazzi, head of the family's bank there, took note of how easy it was to see off a political leader. Republican values might have more pull in a town like Florence, which already enjoyed the collective illusion that it was the modern manifestation of antique glory. So small in stature that he was generally known as Franceschino, this particular Pazzi was renowned for his bad temper and good luck. The Medici had already alienated their main client, the pope. They had alienated the king of Naples. They had alienated all those republican Florentines who believed in the Council of the People and the Council of the Commune. Most of all, Lorenzo de' Medici would never let the Pazzi family back into public life in Florence. If Lorenzo and his brother were killed, the Pazzi bank—which, like so many others, was going through hard times—would be in a position to take over a large part of the Medici's business. Money would bring power.

Franceschino drew in Archbishop Salviati in Pisa and Girolamo Riario, the pope's nephew, now running Imola and eager to build up a serious dukedom before his uncle departed this world. The conspiracy could count on the military support of the Papal States and of Naples. Uncle Iacopo, however, the patrician head of the Pazzi family, a great blasphemer and gambler but highly respected all the same, was reluctant. The stakes were high and the odds poor. For a long time he argued against the assassination attempt. But eventually he came on board. Hadn't Franceschino, he later justified himself, always been the lucky one?

Only two important members of the Pazzi family were not involved in the plot. Guglielmo Pazzi, Lorenzo's brother-in-law, was not even approached. His loyalty would be divided. Renato Pazzi, on the other hand, reputedly the brains of the family, simply thought that murder was unnecessary. The Medici bank was in desperate straits. The best way to destroy Lorenzo would be to lend him money and watch him waste it. His debts would overwhelm him. Renato, then, believed that the Medici's political prominence still depended on the bank. The family's identification with the Florentine state was not complete. They were not, that is, in a position where they could just collect taxes for themselves to pay off their debts.

What did the Pazzi really know about the Medici's financial troubles? In 1475, the Bruges branch had lost a legal battle against ex-London manager Gherardo Canigiani. This was public knowledge. Furious that Canigiani had used Medici money to become an English gentleman, Tommaso Portinari had invited him to act as agent for the bank and buy a shipload of English wool to send to Florence. As soon as the wool was safe at sea,

Portinari refused to pay for it, claiming that Canigiani owed the Medici this and more. "Not even a Turk would behave so," Canigiani protested, and, playing the card of his friendship with King Edward IV, managed to get an agent of the bank imprisoned and eventually to recover his money. Edward still owed the Medici around 30,000 florins.

The murder of Galeazzo Sforza, it was obvious to everybody, would make the chances of the Medici's recovering the huge debts owed by that family even more remote. Galeazzo left an infant son and a shaky maternal regency that was constantly threatened by Galeazzo's ambitious brother, Lodovico. Milan, Francesco Pazzi reckoned, would not be able to help Lorenzo in a crisis.

Then the death in yet another reckless battle, of rash Charles of Burgundy—this only three weeks after Galeazzo Sforza's murder—was evidently another serious blow to the Medici bank. This was January 1477. Even assuming that Charles's family were able to succeed to his dukedom, they wouldn't want to pay off their debts in the near future. The director of the Pazzi bank in Bruges, Pierantonio di Bandini Baroncelli, was a close relative of Tommaso Portinari's young wife, Maria di Bandini Baroncelli. They lived in the same small Italian community in a foreign town. If Pierantonio didn't know that Tommaso was looking at overall losses of 100,000 florins—a vast sum—he certainly would have been aware that things were getting desperate. In the end, it was another close relative of Pierantonio's, Bernardo di Bandini Baroncelli, who struck the first blow against Giuliano de' Medici during mass in the *duomo* fifteen months after the duke of Burgundy's death. More than anything else, it was the murder of Giuliano that saved the Medici bank and set it up for another fourteen years of Lorenzo's mismanagement.

Girolamo Riario lent Francesco Pazzi his personal *condottiere,* Count Montesecco. They plotted. But Lorenzo refused their invitation down to Rome. He was suspicious. Where could they kill him then, and when and how? They must act soon, before someone got wind of the plot. In April 1478, the seventeen-year-old Cardinal Raffaele Riario (nephew to the lord of Imola and great-nephew to the pope—in short, nepotism incarnate) was visiting Florence. Armed men could be sent to the city as his escort. The Medici brothers had offered the child cardinal a celebratory lunch at their villa in Fiesole. The two could be murdered there. But Giuliano didn't turn up for the party. There was no point, the conspirators had all agreed, in killing one brother without the other.

So the appointment with death was set back a week, to another Sunday lunch, after mass, at the Palazzo Medici in town, where the juvenile cardinal was now invited to inspect *Il Magnifico's* famous collection of cameos. For all the animosity between the families, it seemed there was no question of renouncing formal visits with all their etiquette. Sometime during the morning, however, it turned out that once again Giuliano wouldn't be eating with his brother. Frantic, the conspirators agreed they must do the deed at mass, only minutes away. But Count Montesecco shook his head. Not in church, he protested. God would see him in church. Did he imagine the Almighty was blind elsewhere? Montesecco had been Lorenzo's designated assassin and was the most professional of the bunch. A key man. All in a hurry—because now it appeared that someone would actually have to go to Giuliano's house and persuade him to come to church—two priests were given Montesecco's brutal job. Nobody appears to have found their willingness strange. One hailed from Volterra and so had good reason to bear Lorenzo a grudge. Meantime, an army of papal soldiers was within striking distance of the town to the south and the archbishop of Pisa, Francesco Salviati, with about thirty armed men from Perugia, set off to take over the Palazzo della Signoria, the seat of Florentine government.

IT WAS ONE of the rules of Florentine republicanism that for their two-month term of government, the eight priors and one *gonfaloniere della giustizia* must spend the whole time together in the Palazzo della Signoria, eating and sleeping included. Looked at this way, eight weeks in power could seem rather a long time, which is perhaps why the Medici so rarely served on the *signoria*. In any event, as luck would have it, the *gonfaloniere* that day, Cesare Petrucci, was the same man who, as captain of Prato, had courageously put down an armed insurrection in 1470. When Salviati came asking for an audience, it took Petrucci just a few moments to appreciate that there was something suspicious about the archbishop's behavior and to have both him and his men locked up.

In the church, too, everything goes wrong. The Medici brothers are standing well apart. At some agreed moment in the liturgy, Francesco Pazzi and Baroncelli simply massacre Giuliano. Why hadn't they been assigned to Lorenzo? Francesco strikes so repeatedly and violently that he stabs himself in the leg and can barely walk. No doubt the packed church is in an uproar. But the two priests have failed to dispatch Lorenzo. *Il Magnifico* draws his sword, runs. Francesco Nori, once would-be inspector of Accerito Portinari's accounts in Milan and now head of the Florence branch of the Medici bank, blocks the path of the assassins. It's unusual to think of a bank manager protecting his boss with his body. Baroncelli stabs him to death. But Lorenzo is already locked in the sacristy. He is safe. Outside, at the city gates, the papal troops have failed to show. In desperation, old Uncle Iacopo takes to his horse yelling, "Liberty!" up and down the streets. The confused crowd is not impressed. In the end, the common people rally to Lorenzo. He speaks from the balcony of his house. He is identified with law and order. It's a huge step toward a Medici dictatorship.

Revenge is rapid and brutal. Archbishop Salviati, Francesco Pazzi, and scores of others, many innocent, are strung from the windows of the Palazzo della Signoria, or in some cases simply tossed to their deaths from the higher floors. Bodies are dragged about the streets, derided and defiled. Only Baroncelli escapes. The young Cardinal Riario is held prisoner; a hostage is essential to discourage the pope from taking revenge on Florentines in Rome. All adult Pazzi males, with the exception of Lorenzo's brother-in-law Guglielmo, are killed or imprisoned. Their children are ordered to change their last name. Their widows and daughters are forbidden to marry. All over Europe, Pazzi assets will be tracked down and confiscated for years to come. The family's name and emblems must be destroyed wherever they are found.

But Lorenzo's troubles are only beginning. The next two years will constitute the great formative crisis of his life. Not only have the fortunes of his bank plummeted, not only have his brother and one of his few efficient business associates been killed, but now the pope excommunicates him and everybody who defends him. Sixtus "fills all Italy," all Europe, with letters aimed at destroying Lorenzo's reputation and denying him support. Then the Papal States and Naples declare war on Florence and move rapidly on the offensive. Only Lorenzo is our enemy, they announce, willing the Florentine people to ditch their leader. But such tactics rarely work. Especially after a failed assassination attempt in church.

If life hasn't prepared Lorenzo to run the family bank, there is probably no one in Italy better trained for a propaganda war. His letters to other heads of state are endless, intimate, and persuasive. This man was brought up on begging letters. Nothing comes more naturally. And he has a remarkable facility with words. In particular, Louis XI of France is encouraged to renew Angevin claims to the crown of Naples. Milan and Venice are called on to stop arguing with each other and send troops. Back home, Sandro Botticelli is employed to fresco the spectacle of the hanged conspirators—not *inside* a building, but on an *outside* wall near the Palazzo della Signoria. And it's the Florentine government that pays the painter, not the Medici. Forty florins. Andrea del Castagno does a similar job on the façade of the Pazzi *palazzo*. "Natural portraits," enthuses the sixteenth-century art historian Vasari, "and hanged upside down by their feet in strange positions, all different and *bellissimi*." Apparently there is no limit to what can be made beautiful in art. The crime and its punishment will be spectacularly present to the public mind long after the corpses have rotted. The sculptor Verrocchio is ordered to make three life-size figures of Lorenzo to be displayed in various churches. What does a city have artists for? What a shame there are no machines to duplicate these works of art, no photographs, no posters.

Meantime, the brilliant poet and personal friend of Lorenzo's, as well as tutor of his children, Angelo Poliziano, is given the task of writing the official version of the conspiracy, portraying the Pazzi and their accomplices in the worst possible light. The model he adopts is Sallust, the same text that the assassins of Sforza had been reading, except that here the conspirators are not given the role of brave republicans and friends of the poor. They are ignorant, selfish, cruel, grasping. Advantage is taken of the printing press, newly arrived in Italy, to have this travesty distributed as widely as possible. Even today, nothing is more swiftly published than the expedient lie. One way or another, Lorenzo will convince the Florentines.

But if the propaganda war is going well at home, the real conflict is another matter. The invading troops advance into Tuscany with relative ease. Clearly, this is not a moment for restructuring the Medici bank, or thinking about the crazy policies that have brought it to its knees. All the company's assets in Rome and Naples have been confiscated, their staff expelled. There is scarcely a branch producing profits. Yet, for Lorenzo, getting hold of money was never easier. Since his father's cousin, Pierfrancesco de' Medici, the bank's second largest shareholder, died in 1476, and since his surviving heirs, Lorenzo and Giovanni, are only fifteen and eleven, *Il Magnifico*, as their financial guardian, holds their fortune for them in thirteen leather bags. On May 1, 1478, he takes 20,000 florins. On May 3, he takes a further 5,000. On June 2, 8,000; August 8, 8,000; August 13, 1,600; September 27, 11,000. That's the lot. Then at some point Lorenzo also begins to procure money, with no official authorization, from the public purse, the state. This is precisely what, until the assassination attempt, Renato Pazzi was convinced he couldn't do. But Renato has been executed now. Lorenzo will take 75,000 florins from the Florentine state over the coming years. He even sinks to begging for cash from his own bank managers. Francesco Sassetti obliges. He has so much stashed away. Tommaso Portinari does not. This personal affront finally opens Lorenzo's eyes as far as Portinari is concerned. He decides to sever the partnership between the families and close the Bruges and Milan branches of the bank.

1479. ONE YEAR after the assassination attempt. Florence lay under interdiction. It was struck by the plague. The local priests were ordered to disobey the pope and bury the dead. The two *condottieri* the city had hired began to argue. Their armies had to be kept apart to stop them from fighting each other. As a result, it was difficult to bring pressure to bear on the enemy. And impossible to write poetry, of course. Even the usually obedient Clarice, now mother of six, rebelled. The family, along with the urbane poet Poliziano as tutor, had been sent into the country for safety. Mother and teacher loathed each other; both wrote to Lorenzo to complain. That man is teaching Giovanni Latin from the heathen classics instead of the holy Psalter! Giovanni was Lorenzo's second son. The boy learns so fast, Poliziano gripes, when his mother is out of the way. It was old-style Christianity against the new eclectic humanism. As when bank managers bitched, Lorenzo didn't know how to respond. Perhaps he actually liked the idea that those subject to him were in disagreement, rather than ganging up to threaten him. Clarice threw the intellectual poet out of the house. She preferred a priest as tutor. Lorenzo was furious but did nothing. Drawing from both sides of the conflict, young Giovanni would one day become the most eclectic, the most humanist, the most nepotist of popes.

In September 1479, the enemy took the fortress of Poggio Imperiale. The fighting season was over, but the following spring there would be nothing between the Neapolitan army and the gates of Florence. The people had now been taxed as much as a people can be, especially when the enemy has suggested that removal of their leader will resolve the problem. The Venetians and the Milanese were more concerned with their own disputes than with producing the kind of military support that might give their official ally a chance of defending itself. What was Lorenzo to do?

The history books argue endlessly over the Medici's commitment or otherwise to a republican model, their plan perhaps to install themselves as hereditary princes. But although noble birth had certainly become part of the family strategy, Lorenzo was too intelligent to imagine that birth would be enough. Money was important, too. But there wasn't much serious money left. What was still possible, though, was the grand gesture, the legitimacy of individual virtuosity, a cocktail of education, glamour, and charisma. In the new world that was coming, the cult of the leader might perhaps replace the legal right of the king. At dawn on December 6, 1479, laden with expensive gifts, Lorenzo set out for Pisa and a sea trip to Naples to negotiate face-to-face with King Ferrante in his own home. Having taken the decision alone, he wrote a moving letter to those who were constitutionally in power, the *signoria,* speaking of his willingness to sacrifice himself for the good of the city. "And with this good intention I set out: that perhaps God wishes that since this war began with the blood of my brother and my own, so too it may end by my hand. . . . For if our adversaries want nothing but me, they shall have me freely in their hands; and if they want something more, then we shall see." The letter was perfectly calculated, and perhaps honest too. No doubt Lorenzo foresaw its appearance in history books.

In his *Storie fiorentine,* Guicciardini remarks that the expensive peace treaty that Lorenzo eventually brought back from Naples could perfectly well have been negotiated without that dangerous visit. Yet one can't help feeling that the drama of the gesture—the just having thought of it and dared it, for there was no classical model—was absolutely central to the image that Lorenzo later created for himself as leader of Florence. Propaganda can invent a great deal, but it does prefer to work with a kernel of truth. Granted, Lorenzo had opened secret negotiations with King Ferrante long before he left; granted, he had various diplomatic cards up his sleeve, concessions to make; but all the same, it was an act of enormous courage to place oneself in the hands of a "most restless, most faithless, most hostile king," a man who not so long ago had promised safe conduct to the *condottiere* Iacopo Piccinino (son of the more famous Niccolò) and then had him put to death on arrival.

Stendhal, in his *Histoire de la Peinture en Italie,* suggests that it was only through the drug of aesthetic passion and pleasure that the Medici were able to subdue the Florentines' "passionate love for liberty and implacable hatred of nobility." They accepted the Medici, that is, because the family filled the city with beautiful things. There may be something in this, but not if we are to limit aesthetics and beauty to canonical works of art. Pictures, sculptures, *palazzi* would never have been enough. Lorenzo had gone into the lion's den. It was a marvelous gesture. Over three long months, he had talked the enemy around. He had seduced King Ferrante. And the drama of it, the magnificence of the adventure, had seduced the Florentines. From now on, they knew that they were governed by a man with balls and charisma. And enormous luck. For in August 1480, the Turkish army landed on the Italian peninsula and seized Otranto on the southeast coast. Twelve thousand people were killed and ten thousand taken into slavery. How all the other wars mentioned in this book pale into insignificance beside these figures. But it was excellent news for Lorenzo. In return for his contribution to the collective effort to repel the Infidel, he could demand the return of territories conceded in his treaty with King Ferrante, as well as complete absolution from the now-nervous Pope Sixtus IV.

So, quite scandalously, everything at last returned to normal, as if the Pazzi conspiracy had never been. In 1478, immediately after the assassination attempt, the Florentine *signoria* had written to Sixtus describing him as "Judas in the seat of Peter." In response, Lorenzo had been condemned as a "heretic," which meant a death sentence. And now, just three years later, all was forgiven and forgotten. In December 1481, Giovanni Tornabuoni was down in Rome again, negotiating recognition of the papal debt to the Medici bank, reassuring old clients, resuming business. Yet something had changed. In letters back to his nephew, Lorenzo, Tornabuoni for the first time switches from the familiar *tu* to the formal *voi,* as if addressing a superior. As head of the bank, Lorenzo had always been addressed as *la Magnificenza vostra*. The same was true of his father, and of Cosimo too in his old age. It was ordinary etiquette. But now, after the feat of Naples, after taking the city's destiny in his own hands and delivering it from its enemies, Lorenzo is suddenly *Il Magnifico*. Out on his own. Everyday politeness is elevated into individual glory. A stiff old uncle bends his knee. At which point, Lorenzo's need for the bank has really ceased to exist. It's unthinkable that *Il Magnifico* might lose power merely for a lack of cash.

BIOGRAPHIES OF LORENZO tend toward hagiography. They concentrate on this period between 1480 and 1492 and describe it as a golden age. Didn't Machiavelli, in the gloom of sixteenth-century foreign dominance, describe it as such? Lorenzo manipulates the available art patronage, private and public, sending great painters hither and thither to those who want the best. He doesn't commission much himself because money is short and he has, as we shall see, other uses for it. When he does spend, it's not on the kind of public and religious projects that Cosimo patronized. Lorenzo's purchases are private. He likes to possess things. On the other hand, he has clearly grasped the idea of using art and even poetry to enhance the reputation of the state and the legitimacy of his reign. The Florentine government would preside over and promote the production of beauty. Such a policy is widely believed to be a good thing. Fortunately, there was a remarkable supply of first-class artists: Ghirlandaio, Verrocchio, Perugino, Pollaiuolo, Botticelli, Leonardo. Fortunately, there were excellent writers—Poliziano, Landino, Lorenzo himself—capable of transforming Tuscan into *the* language of Italy, a coup beyond any military victory.

And he is praised for his diplomacy. He became "almost the balance of all Italy," said Guicciardini, meaning that Lorenzo preserved the balance of power. Later biographers take up the expression without the *almost*. Lorenzo opposed Venice in its expansionist assault on Ferrara in the early 1480s; he opposed Pope Innocent VIII's expansionist assault on Naples in the mid-eighties; but he moved more carefully now, choosing to alienate no one over the long run, offering favors to everybody. As the weakest of the five Italian powers, Lorenzo had an obvious interest in maintaining the status quo. Unable to shine militarily, his city must stand out for its artistic achievements. What was expedient then is understood as virtuous now.

Or the biographies are written in indignant opposition to the hagiographies, in much the same way that many citizens of Florence hated Lorenzo more intensely the more the world praised him. On his return from Naples, almost the first thing Lorenzo undertook was another and final reform of the state. A new constitutional body of only seventy chosen Medici supporters was given huge powers. Every vote against Lorenzo was always a personal affront. Every picture commissioned took into account the political loyalties of the painter, the propaganda value of the image. Speaking of the need for peace, Lorenzo missed no opportunity to expand Florence's borders. In 1484, on the slightest of pretexts, the garrison town of Pietrasanta was seized from the Genoese. Writing convincingly of the need for free choice in marriage, he imposed brides on reluctant spouses. He betrothed his fourteen-year-old daughter Maddalena to the illegitimate, debauched, and drunken son of Pope Sixtus's successor, Innocent VIII. The rhetoric of fiscal equality ever on his lips, he introduced a new coin, the *quattrino bianco,* in which all customs duties must be paid. The silver *picciolo* had long been losing value. The new money effectively increased those taxes paid by the poor by 25 percent. It did not alter their incomes.

Complaining of the heavy responsibilities of power, he exercised it ever more determinedly, "holding the city completely in his will as if he were a prince waving a baton," says Guicciardini. Rushing out of the Palazzo della Signoria one January morning in 1489, four days after his fortieth birthday, Lorenzo waves his now-gouty arm to silence the crowd. They are demanding that a certain criminal should be spared execution. Hang him *now,* Lorenzo orders, here. The man had killed a police agent. The man is hanged. Four protesters are whipped and banished. Lorenzo has a considerable investment in the powers of the police. He goes nowhere now without an armed bodyguard of a dozen men, paid for by the state.

Lorenzo is a tyrant and the Pazzi conspirators were republican martyrs. Such was the burden of Alamanno Rinuccini's *Dialogue on Liberty,* written, in the classical style, when its author retired to his country villa in 1479, during the war with Naples and the pope. With the state of Medici tyranny, he wrote, the only thing an honest man can do is to withdraw from public life. Rinuccini had a long record of holding high offices under the Medici, to whom he dedicated various translations from the Greek; but he had fallen out with Lorenzo and his life savings had been held in the Pazzi bank. Nevertheless, shortly after writing the dialogue, which he was wise enough not to publish, he went back to Florence and served the Medici regime in a variety of public offices for many years.

The ambiguity of the case is emblematic. Was the core of Rinuccini's personality in his denunciation of the Medici? Or was there an element of sour grapes and rhetorical exercise? Was the man's public service a sad charade that served to prop up a dangerous tyrant? Or was it honorable and a pleasure? "So many men on the councils denounce the Medici over dinnertime discussion at home in their villas," wrote Marco Parenti, "then vote as they're told when they are back in Florence." It seemed a new sort of personality was in the making: that of the man who does not find it too much of a problem to be liberal and virtuous in private while toeing an authoritarian line in public. And perhaps this had come about in response to a new kind of society where public life would always involve a surrender of honesty, if only because the basis of power would always be suspect, always require a constant effort of propaganda to assert its legitimacy. In these murky circumstances, hardly unfamiliar to us today, to write hagiography or its opposite is to miss the point.

LORENZO WAS NOW so suspicious of all and sundry that he routinely had official Florentine ambassadors in foreign courts shadowed and duplicated by his own personal spies. Yet his trust in his bank managers seemed unbounded. The overall director, Francesco Sassetti, a man quite incapable of taking unpleasant decisions, was left entirely to his own devices, despite the fact that he worked from Lorenzo's house in Florence. In Rome, Uncle Giovanni Tornabuoni swung from gloom to optimism with no long-term vision, no flexibility. "The pope is as stubborn as a corpse," he complained of Innocent's unwillingness to repay his debts. Yet Tornabuoni continued to tie up most of the bank's capital with the Curia. In Bruges, before the final showdown, Tommaso Portinari had actually managed to persuade Lorenzo to form a separate company for the only profitable business the branch was doing, the occasional importation of English wool. Since Portinari had a larger share in this company than in the bank, he took a bigger slice of the gains, while losing a smaller percentage on the branch's overall losses. "He took advantage of my inexperience," Lorenzo later complained. But *Il Magnifico* had been running the Florentine Republic for years at the time, and a child would have understood the mathematics of the deal.

An atmosphere of farce hangs over these last years of the

Medici bank. A second generation of untouchables and prima donnas was now being trained up beneath the first. In Bruges, Antonio de' Medici, a distant cousin of Lorenzo's, was so arrogant that when the family promoted him to deputy director, the other employees threatened a walkout and he had to be recalled to Florence. Later, Antonio would be sent to Constantinople to negotiate, successfully, the extradition of Giuliano's assassin, Bernardo di Bandini Baroncelli. In Lyon, Lionetto de' Rossi, Lorenzo's brother-in-law, was convinced that one of his staff, Cosimo Sassetti, son of the general director, had been sent to spy on him. Most likely he had; Lionetto, after all, had been writing the most insulting things about the boy's father in vitriolic letters to Lorenzo. Fortunately, the young Sassetti was as credulous as he was offensive. Overwhelmed by losses from bad loans, Lionetto sent Cosimo back to Florence with a balance sheet reporting profits. The director's son was the only one taken in. Arriving in Lyon to investigate, in 1485, a certain Lorenzo Spinelli wrote to Lorenzo to say that Lionetto was completely out of his mind.

The bank was paying the price for its fatal attraction to political power. To lend to people whose reputation and position do not depend on honoring their debts will always be dangerous, but to give huge sums to people who actually feel it is *undignified* to repay is madness. These were not the kind of people you could take to court. They *were* the court. Often a condition of lending to one of them was that you must not lend to another. Louis XI of France was furious that the Medici were financing his enemy Charles the Bold, and so took measures against the bank in Lyon. Tornabuoni, angry that the French branch wasn't sending him the money for papal bulls, refused to honor an important letter of credit from

Hans Memling's The Last Judgment *(detail), commissioned by Tommaso Portinari. Despite losing 100,000 florins for the Medici bank, Tommaso instructs the great painter to imagine how the Angel of Death will weigh him in the balance when the bottom line is finally drawn.*

Lyon. The bank's reputation could only plummet. The Florence branch started trading silk with a separate, non-Medici agent in the French town. At least they knew they would be paid. Lionetto was furious. How can I ever get my branch back into profit if the others take their business elsewhere? Far too late, Lorenzo sweetly invited his brother-in-law back to Florence to discuss matters, and on his arrival had him arrested and thrown in a debtors' jail.

It wasn't the first time. Returning to Florence after the closure of the London office in 1480, Tommaso Guidetti had been arrested on the request of the Venice branch of the bank. He had not paid them for a shipload of currants. The debt amounted to more than 3,500 florins. I paid Tommaso Portinari in Bruges, was Guidetti's claim. It was feasible. All the same, he had to flee from Florence, leaving behind a teenage wife, pregnant. The case was still unsettled more than thirty years later.

But a considerable number of court cases were now underway. Lorenzo was being pursued for the money he had taken from his young cousins, the two sons of Pierfrancesco de' Medici. In 1485, the precious country villas had to be sold to make amends. It was a huge loss of prestige. The legal battle over the seizure of the Bruges galleys would go on into the second decade of the next century. With justice on his mind, Tommaso Portinari had Hans Memling paint him kneeling, naked, on one side of a pair of giant weighing scales held up by a great black Angel of Death. It is extraordinary that the Last Judgment scene, the final assessment of a man's moral worth, something that had been so disturbing to the merchants of Cosimo's time, should have become a vehicle for this sort of confident exhibitionism, as if the man were quite sure he was on his way to paradise. Weighing up Portinari's performance in Bruges, Lorenzo calculated a loss of 70,000 florins. "Such are the great earnings that the management of Tommaso Portinari has brought," he noted ironically. He was wrong. Losses were well over 100,000 florins.

Avignon closed down in 1478. Likewise Milan. The famous *palazzo* was sold. One of the two wool workshops had already gone. The silk workshop closed in 1480. That same year, the London and Bruges branches with all their debts were formally handed over to Portinari. Venice closed in 1481. In 1482, a proposal for restructuring the whole bank was drawn up. There would be two holdings, one under Tornabuoni, running Rome and Naples, the other under Sassetti, running Florence, Lyon, and Pisa. Two barons, two entirely separate entities to satisfy two considerable egos. Total capital would be only about 52,000 florins, of which Lorenzo's part was under 20,000, the merest trifle compared with the vast sums he had inherited. Nothing became of the plan. Nothing was done to coordinate the remaining branches or to have their directors care about each other's losses. Making no serious contribution to economic activity, serving only to finance wars and the consumption of luxury goods on the part of a debt-ridden aristocracy, the Medici bank continued its inglorious decline through those years that would soon be referred to as "golden." Pisa closed in 1489. Which left just Florence, Rome, Naples, and Lyon.

FORTUNATELY, THERE WERE other things for bankers to do aside from banking. Cosimo had used his staff to hunt down ancient manuscripts. Piero had bought paintings, tapestries, ponies for the kids. After 1483, Lorenzo began to send his bank managers on a hunt for lucrative Church appointments for his fourth child and second son, Giovanni, who had just received the tonsure and ordination into the priesthood. He was eight years old. Almost immediately, the Lyon branch of the bank entered into negotiations that would make the boy abbot of Fontdouce in western France. Later he acquired the priory of Saint Gemme, near Chartres. Ecclesiastical incomes were steady and risk-free. The monks of the Abbey of Le Pin, near Poitiers, barricaded themselves inside when Cosimo Sassetti arrived with orders to take possession in the name of the infant bishop. Having lost so much through banking, Lorenzo had finally found a way of making money in which he excelled. It was a question of connections, favors, gifts, promises. One by one the Church benefices fell into his son's lap: the Abbey of Passignano on the road to Siena, churches in Prato, the Arno Valley, the Mugello; the Abbey of Monte Cassino near Naples, Morimondo, near Milan. By the time the bank collapsed, the Church incomes would be there to give the family a new economic base.

It was a policy that required the investment of whatever resources Lorenzo could muster. As with every project, he was ambitious. Shortly after marrying off his young daughter Maddalena to the pope's dissolute son, he had the bank lend the Curia 30,000 florins. This was stretching credit to the limit. He accepted alum instead of cash for arrears repayments on papal loans, though the Medici no longer held the monopoly on merchandising alum and had few outlets from which they could sell the mineral. Every diplomatic courier traveling from Florence to

Rome starts to bring gifts for Pope Innocent. Apparently the pontiff loves to eat game. Then ply him with game. He loves wine. Here are eighteen flasks of finest Vernaccia. And beautiful fabrics. And the best artists. Anything that will make His Holiness happy. "The pope sleeps with Lorenzo *il Magnifico*'s eyes," commented a delegate from Ferrara. Until at last the seduction was complete. In 1489, the pope caved in, waived age restrictions, and made the thirteen-year-old Giovanni di Lorenzo de' Medici a cardinal. Now he could accumulate even more benefices. "The greatest honor ever conferred upon our house," Lorenzo announced. Cardinal Giovanni de' Medici, later Pope Leo X, would keep the Medici fortunes alive after their expulsion from Florence in 1494 until their return in 1512.

BUT THE CHURCH was not entirely rotten. While the Medici were seeking to consolidate the family's temporal power through acquiring Church incomes, *Il Magnifico*'s near-contemporary, Girolamo Savonarola, was climbing the ecclesiastical hierarchy in an entirely different spirit. Like the young Giovanni, Savonarola too would one day be offered a cardinal's hat. And as with Giovanni, the appointment, or rather its offer, came as part of a bargain, an exchange, as though Church appointments were a recognized form of currency. With Giovanni, the honor constituted a payment for favors the Medici had already granted to pope and Church; in Savonarola's case, the offer of the cardinalship was conditional on his granting a favor to Rome in the future: He must moderate his inflammatory preaching, he must get back into line, he must stop behaving as if he were in direct contact with God and holier than the official Church. Savonarola refused. "I don't want any hats," he replied to the pope, "nor mitres great or small; the only thing I want is what you gave your saints: death. A red hat, a hat of blood, that's what I desire."

Savonarola was the antithesis of Lorenzo and of the Medici and bankers in general. Here, at last, was a man who wouldn't trade, a man who had no use for the art of exchange, who couldn't be seduced. Yet, like Lorenzo, Savonarola was an artist, and in his own way a showman. His terrifying sermons of gloom and doom, of the need for radical spiritual renewal, transformed the Florence of Lorenzo's and the Medici bank's last years, setting *Il Magnifico*'s ethos and achievements in sharp and twilit relief.

It had taken medieval Christianity a thousand years to produce the cautious revolution that was humanism, a movement eager to escape Christianity's straitjacket, but careful never to renounce its principles. It took eclectic humanism only a hundred years to provoke the reaction that was Savonarola. But from the moment the secular began to creep into the sacred space, the bankers to gratify their vanity in altarpieces and tombs, the cardinals to collect their "discretionary" returns on deposits, the popes to mix up myth and prayer book—not to mention holy wars and commercial monopolies—Savonarola and, soon after him, Luther were figures in the making, men formed in opposition to a Church authority that was seen as corrupt; fundamentalists. Unlike the early Christians, they did not call their followers out of the world to a radically separate life. Instead, they demanded that official and powerful Christendom become truly Christian. The political consequences of such a transformation, should it ever take place, were enormous.

Born in Ferrara in 1452, called away from a career in medicine by a verse from *Genesis*—"Get thee out of thy country!"—Savonarola first preached in Florence between 1482 and 1487. "He introduced almost a new way of pronouncing God's word, Apostolic, without dividing up the sermon, not proposing questions and answers, never singing, avoiding ornament and eloquence. His aim was just to expound something from the Old Testament and introduce the simplicity of the early church. . . ."

Thus the comment of a contemporary. It was not, then, a return to medieval Christian preaching. The negatives in this description tell us that. There would be no old-style scholastic caviling. But neither would there be pretty quotations from classical authors, nor any reference to authorities outside the word of God. In a society buzzing with too many ideas, a Church cluttered with pricey secular bric-a-brac, Savonarola strips his Christianity down to the bare scriptures, the naked crucifix. "I sense a light within me," he says. It is Christ, the light of the world. But not, as Ficino would have it, Plato's light, or Proclus's, or that of some Orphic hymn. "Oh priests, oh prelates of the Church of Christ," cries Savonarola, "leave your benefices, which you cannot justly hold, leave your pomp, your splendid feasts and banquets." He might have been preaching directly to Giovanni de' Medici. Lorenzo also warned his son not to be corrupted by that "pit of iniquity" that was Rome. But there was no question of abandoning the benefices. Why else did one go into the Church?

The contrast alerts us to a condition essential to the develop-

Savonarola, as portrayed by Fra Bartolomeo. The austere lines and sharp contrasts underline the man's unswerving devotion and refusal to compromise. Finally, the Medici had met someone who could not be bought.

ment of international banks of the Medici variety: a certain laxity in the application of religious law, or, better still, a complete separation of church and state. In short, there is an affinity between money and eclecticism. "No man can serve two masters," says Jesus. But money can serve any number. It is no respecter of principles. Broken up into discreet and neutral units, value flows into any cup, a shower of gold into any coffer, be it in Constantinople, Rome, or Jerusalem. The alum merchant trades with the Turk. The silk manufacturer is happy to sell provocative clothes to the pretty ladies of Florence. The idealist, whether Christian or Muslim, Communist or No-Global, must always be suspicious of money and banking. But the idealist is not to be confused with the ideas man. Quite the contrary. Admirably flexible, the humanist thinkers with their eclectic reading were notorious for finding authorities to justify whatever form of government best suited their paymasters. In 1471, Bartolomeo dedicated his treatise, "On the Prince," to Federico Gonzaga. In 1475, the same text reappeared as "On the Citizen," dedicated to Lorenzo de' Medici. In the same period, depending upon which patrons were paying him, Francesco Patrizi wrote "On Republican Education" and then "On the Kingdom and Education of Kings." Both systems were best. Money has a way of being right. Only popular government by the poor is unforgivable.

Spiritual renewal can only come through poverty, Savonarola preached, through an end to the clergy's collusion with wealth and power. His would not be a church that worked with banks. Largely ignored, the monk left Florence in 1487. Meanwhile, the great political upheavals of his career behind him, Lorenzo was writing poetry again: cycles of love poems, dense with labored references to classical myth but lightened by marvelous landscape description. Busy with his verses, *Il Magnifico* ignored a proposal from Lorenzo Spinelli, the new director in Lyon, to revive the Medici bank's old holding structure. Lorenzo himself was one of the bank's main debtors now, one of the political leaders who would never repay. In 1488, a ban on public festivities in Florence, something that had been in force since the Pazzi conspiracy ten years ago, was finally lifted. Is it a coincidence that Lorenzo's wife, Clarice, had succumbed to tuberculosis that same summer? Lorenzo was away at the thermal baths when she died. He wrote no poem for her. But for the first celebration of Carnival after a decade's break, he produced some new Carnival songs, and some moving lyrics about youth. The loves of Bacchus and Ariadne are evoked to remind the adolescents of Florence to seize the day:

Quanto è bella giovinezza,	How fine youth is
che si fugge tutta via	Though it flee away
Chi vuole essere lieto, sia,	Let he who wishes, enjoy
di doman non c'è certezza	Nothing's certain tomorrow

Stiff in the joints though he now was, Lorenzo practiced what he preached and got on his horse at night to visit Bartolomea de' Nasi when she was away from her husband in her country villa. "Crazy," writes Guicciardini, "to think that a man of such reputation and prudence, forty years old, was so taken by a woman, hardly beautiful and full of years, as to do things that would have seemed dishonest to every youngster."

Yet eclecticism and promiscuity are always vulnerable to a nostalgia for rigid principles, as the moneyed classes yearn for a value that can't be counted. The brilliant Pico della Mirandola, master of many languages, lover of the mystics and the Kabbalah, was impressed by Savonarola's preaching, by his strict attention to the words of the biblical text. Bring him back to Florence, he told Lorenzo, he'll be an asset. Suffering severely from gout, aware that his own death couldn't be far off, Lorenzo was persuaded. He and Pico couldn't have known that Girolamo was now in a decidedly visionary mood, having convinced himself he was a reincarnation of the Old Testament prophets he had studied for so long. On August 1, 1490, in San Marco, the monastery that Cosimo had had rebuilt, Savonarola began his series of sermons on the Apocalypse. He had three basic themes: The need for Church renewal; the belief that before renewal God would punish all Italy with some terrible catastrophe; the conviction that this must happen soon.

What could such a prediction mean but the end of Medici rule? In Lent of 1491, Savonarola preached what he himself described as *terrifica praedicatio*—a terrifying sermon. Despite invitations from both the *signoria* and the Church authorities to take it easy, he repeated his themes again and again. This disaster will happen very soon. Had he seen the Medici's balance sheets? Cardinal Giovanni was already living far beyond his means, borrowing from the bank to the tune of 7,000 florins. Sassetti was dead. Tornabuoni and Spinelli were desperate. With the general decline of trade, the English refusal to export their raw wool, almost all the other Florentine banks had gone under.

In April, Savonarola preached to the priors in Palazzo della Signoria. He condemned Lorenzo's tyranny. He condemned corruption. Those on the losing side of the Medici regime flocked to hear him. The poor were enchanted. Oppressed by asthma and arthritis, Lorenzo couldn't persuade the priest to compromise, or even to talk to him in person. The eclectic tries to include the fundamentalist in his collection, his entourage of artists, philosophers, poets; the banker seeks to finance him, to count him among his debtors; but the fundamentalist won't have it.

In July 1491, Savonarola is elected prior of San Marco. He takes the cell at the opposite end of the monastery from Cosimo's. There are no pretty paintings. "The real preacher," he says, "cannot flatter a prince, only attack his vices." Clearly this man is an opponent of a quite different caliber from the debt-ridden Innocent, the murderous Sixtus. Even good Archbishop Antonino, in Cosimo's time, was always open to compromise. But Savonarola preaches values that are beyond money's grasp. He yearns for poverty, even death. It's a showdown.

Near death himself, Lorenzo begins to write religious hymns. As always, he is master of form and content, conversant with his predecessors, intimate and seductive. Some of the hymns are written to be sung to the same tunes as the bawdy Carnival songs. At the same time he presses on with his *Commentary on My Sonnets,* a long work in which he rearranges the old love poems to Lucrezia in a prose analysis that offers an imaginary autobiography of unhappy love and Platonic transcendence. Supremely self-conscious, even in the grip of terminal illness, Lorenzo is still performing.

On April 5, 1492, lightning strikes the dome of the *duomo*. "Behold," preaches Savonarola, "swift and sudden the sword of the Lord upon our land." Only three days later, religious prophecy and Renaissance theatricality come together in the perfect deathbed scene. At his last gasp, kissing a silver crucifix encrusted with precious stones, Lorenzo calls for Savonarola.

Was this a victory or a defeat? From Giovanni di Bicci's first contracts with the Curia, Cosimo's supervision of the design of Giovanni XXIII's tomb, the history of the Medici bank had always been intertwined with that of the Church. They were two institutions that repelled and attracted each other, came together and fell apart, in one drama after another. Exiled, Cosimo had hidden his money in churches; almost all his patronage had favored religious buildings, devotional paintings. The same was true of his great director Giovanni Benci. "Should pay up by John the Baptist's Day," was a typical comment in bank correspondence. Interest on loans accumulated from one martyr's festival to the next. "In the name of God and of Profit," announced the account books. And as the decades passed, Medici employees all over Europe had poured the bank's money into chapels and churches. Lorenzo had almost been murdered in church. Wounded by two priests, he had fought one pope, flattered another, and finally brought family and church together in a son who was already on his way to squandering what was left of the family resources, as one day he would ruin the finances of the Curia.

Now Savonarola meets Lorenzo at death's door. Lorenzo has already been granted extreme unction—the last rites of the

Church—so the priest has no power over his eternal soul. On the other hand, he can hardly refuse the invitation to speak to a dying man. If you recover, you must change your life, Savonarola says. Knowing there is no recovery, Lorenzo agrees. Savonarola gives his blessing. It's a standoff, a stalemate, an insoluble antagonism: money and metaphysics, eclectic humanism and rigid fundamentalism. The wonder is that history should offer us an encounter so emblematic of the forces whose clash will decide the future of Europe. Twenty-five years later, Giovanni de' Medici's frank enjoyment of the papacy would be challenged by the revolt of Martin Luther. Banking would be profoundly affected. Protestant England was the first to legalize usury. Catholic Italy, under the Counter-Reformation, reimposed the old laws that bred the old subterfuges.

HOW DIFFICULT TO be Piero di Lorenzo de' Medici! "I have three sons," Lorenzo is reputed to have said, "one dumb, one smart, one sweet." Piero was the dumb one, Giovanni the smart. If the authority of Lorenzo had depended first on wealth, later on charisma, Piero possessed neither. The money had mostly been spent, and there are cases where even the best education is just wasted time. Piero was good at sports, particularly an early form of football. But the era of the sports celebrity had not yet arrived. He had inherited Lorenzo's suspicious nature but not his charm. And yet, remarks Guicciardini, the succession was so smooth, "the good will on the part of people and princes so great, that had

Piero had even an ounce of wit and prudence, he could not have fallen." He didn't and he fell.

Throughout the fifteenth century, it had been the habit of the Italian city-states, at some crisis point in their internal struggles, to play the threatening card of calling on a foreign ally to tip the balance in the peninsula. In desperate straits against Rome and Naples in 1480, Florence had invited the French to reconsider their claims to the throne of Naples. In 1482, during the Venetian assault on Ferrara, Florence and Milan had encouraged the Turks to step up their attacks on Venice's maritime possessions. Venice had replied by inviting the duke of Lorraine to consider *his* claim to Naples, the duke of Orleans his to Milan. In a pointless war against Naples in 1483, Pope Innocent VIII had again suggested that the duke of Lorraine might want to take the kingdom. Dangerous games. Nobody seems to have considered what might actually happen if a foreign army did push into Italy. It was Piero's bad luck to find out.

Ignoring the bank, rapidly alienating Florence's patrician families, Piero also infuriated Lodovico Sforza, now duke of Milan, by appearing to prefer the city's other ally, Naples. All too soon, Sforza was inviting the king of France to consider himself king of Naples. In Paris, young Charles VIII had only just shaken off an oppressive regency and come into his own. He wanted to do something bold. And he did. He gathered 30,000 men and marched over the Alps, down through Lombardy, heading south.

Allied to Naples, Florence was a potential target for this campaign. Suddenly an army far bigger than any the Florentines had had to deal with in recent decades was heading toward the city, an army with a foreign king at its head, not a paid Italian *condottiere* who might be bribed. In desperation, as the French approached and with the city's political class almost entirely against him, Piero tried to repeat the gesture his father had made when he went to Naples to deal face-to-face with King Ferrante more than a decade ago. But the boy was only twenty-two. He hadn't prepared the ground. It was the gesture of a novice trying to copy the maestro's masterpiece. He even repeated the same charade of leaving the town first and sending back a letter to be read to the *signoria*.

I won't sack Florence if you hand over Sarazana, Sarzanello, Pietrasanta, and the ports of Pisa and Leghorn: those were the French king's conditions. He was demanding more or less all of Florence's gains over the last century. To everybody's surprise, Piero agreed. The *signoria* was furious and refused to recognize the agreement. It was a crucial break, a reminder that constitutional power did not lie with the Medici. The *signoria* sent out Savonarola to talk to Charles, the irony being that Savonarola actually welcomed the French arrival. This foreign army was the fulfillment of all his prophecies of doom.

Piero returned to Florence on November 8. The next day, in an apparently unplanned incident, someone decided to bar the doors to the *signoria* when he arrived there with a number of armed men. In a matter of hours, the town was in an uproar, the cries of "*popolo*" and "*libertà*" had begun. Piero panicked, got on his horse, and headed out of town. The Palazzo Medici was sacked. Suddenly the silk sheets, the precious sculptures, the painted reliquaries were being dragged out into the street. A hundred years of careful accumulation was lost in a matter of hours. On November 10, the very day after Piero's departure, all Medici innovations in the republic's constitution were dismantled, all Medici enemies exiled since 1434 were recalled; the hated new heavyweight coin for customs taxes was abolished, and, of course, the Medici bank and all its assets were confiscated. To have moved so fast, there must have been those who couldn't wait to see the back of the family. A month later, Savonarola declared Jesus Christ king of Florence, as if the Savior himself had pushed over the bank's changing tables.

It wouldn't last. In 1498, accused of heresy by the official Church and abandoned by much of his congregation, Savonarola was burned at the stake. Fundamentalism is one thing in the pulpit, another in government. And fourteen years later, having finally infiltrated to the highest levels the institution that had been the source of so much of their wealth, the Medici returned to Florence on the back of Vatican power and overturned the republic. In 1529, they were officially recognized as dukes and ready to serve the Counter-Reformation in that long war of retrenchment that would keep an imitation of the older world—complete with those two complicit conundrums, the divine right of princes and the temporal power of the Church—in suffocating place for more than three hundred years.

These new Medici of the sixteenth and seventeenth centuries ordered monuments of tax-funded magnificence to establish an aura of legitimacy. All the fruitful ambiguity that had characterized old Cosimo's commissions, all the urgent tension between money and metaphysics, was gone. With the grand dukes of Tuscany, we are in the world of larger-than-life equestrian statues, flattering official portraits, imagined military glory, and extravagant, though always breathtaking mannerism. In such circumstances, there was no need to revive the bank. In fact, the sooner people forgot that the family had ever sat behind their tables in via Porta Rossa, copying down the details of dubious exchange deals, the better.

Bibliographic Notes

Exercising power to which no one in Florence was constitutionally entitled, the Medici of the fifteenth century were obliged to be great propagandists, to present themselves as special, gifted, worthy. Perhaps this is one reason why there is such an extraordinary amount of literature about them. There are those historians who buy into the Medici's flattering vision of themselves, those who react and reject, and those who try to sort out the wood from the trees. Nothing breeds interest like an ongoing argument.

Most modern readers will come to the subject through the more popular books, such as Christopher Hibbert's *The Rise and Fall of the House of Medici,* or J. R. Hale's *Florence and the Medici: The Pattern of Control*. Hibbert's book invests enthusiastically in the Medici myth and is the kind of thing tourists are reading while visiting the Uffizi gallery and generally falling in love with Renaissance Florence. In fact, it can be found stacked up in many of the city's museum bookshops. It's fun but not always accurate. Just as readable, but less colorful and more credible, Hale pays the price for his sobriety by not being so widely available.

The more academic the book, the more likely it is to be resisting the myth and looking for an ugly truth. Lauro Martines's *Power and Imagination: City-States in Renaissance Italy,* gives really excellent background to the Medici story, but Martines is not one to allow special pleading and condemns the banking family as the ruin of Florentine republicanism. He has recently tried to popularize this view in the highly readable *April Blood: Florence and the Plot against the Medici,* where he argues that all in all it would have been a good thing if the Pazzi family had managed to murder Lorenzo *il Magnifico* in the *duomo* in 1478. Martines is a moralist who likes to be out on a limb but is nonetheless interesting for that.

Il Magnifico tends to form a subject all on his own, and here the popular books presently in print are Cecilia Ady's *Lorenzo de' Medici* and Antonio Altomonte's *Il Magnifico*. Both are in the business of glorification but well worth reading as long as you keep a pinch of salt about you. Jack Lang's more recent biography, *Il Magnifico,* is less attractive and even less believable. Once France's minister for education, Lang seems determined not to consult the vast amount of American scholarship that has been done on the Medici since World War II; as a result, a lot of what he says about the Medici bank's fortunes under Lorenzo doesn't add up.

Which brings us to the heavier stuff. The Florentines were committed bureaucrats and the city's archives still house the tax returns of the fifteenth century, the minutes of thousands of government committee meetings, lists upon lists of those eligible for office at different levels in the different quarters and districts, and so on. The City Council of Florence has recently put all these archives up on the Web for general public inspection, but alas, what you see is facsimiles of the originals. Even if you are familiar with the Italian and Latin of the time, the handwriting is more or less illegible and the material can't be searched by just typing in a name and calling up all the places it occurs. No, to tackle the archives would require several lifetimes of total dedication. So you're obliged to go to the scholars.

Nicolai Rubenstein's book *The Government of Florence Under the Medici* is as essential as it is infuriating. Rubenstein brings together decades of meticulous scholarship and is admirably impartial as he analyzes how exactly the Medici manipulated the Florentine constitution. Unfortunately, he leaves certain crucial explanations of the workings of that constitution until deep into the book. Often whole chapters begin to make sense only when you discover a footnote on page two hundred and something with the vital piece of information. This is only for the seriously committed.

The same goes for Raymond de Roover's *The Rise and Decline of the Medici Bank, 1397–1494*. Of all the books you can read on the Medici, Roover's has the most extraordinary facts, but they are hidden away among balance sheets, reflections on accounting practices, considerations of trade patterns, and so on. Curiously, there is almost no overlap between these two monumental works, as if the Medici had split their political and commercial lives quite drastically, something that is hard to believe.

More recently, the historian Dale Kent has added a third dimension to this Medici duality with her meticulously researched book *Cosimo de' Medici and the Florentine Renaissance*. This gives an exhaustive account of all the artworks and buildings that Cosimo may or may not have commissioned, the nature of his involvement, and the context in which it all took place. Kent lets herself get drawn into a lot of sterile argument with other academics about the nature of Cosimo's intentions, but the book is absolutely fascinating, assuming you have oceans of time on your hands.

Enough. There are scores of relevant books, literally hundreds of collections of learned articles—on Florentine dress, on the changing nature of exile in the 1500s, the sumptuary laws, the voyages of the trading galleys. As you proceed, you realize how many of the texts contradict each other, even on matters of bare fact, and how elusive any definitive vision of the Medicis must be. At this point, my advice is to stop worrying too much about "the truth" and to go back to what material from the time is still available and readable. Machiavelli's *Florentine Histories* is a joy, and Francesco Guicciardini's various historical accounts likewise. Both were written in the early sixteenth century. Then there are Lorenzo *il Magnifico*'s clever poems, Savonarola's solemn sermons, Ficino's bizarre Platonist reflections. The web of ideas soon grows thick indeed. What you are looking at is the birth throes of our modern mindset.

In conclusion, if you want to check out someone who had the talent and imagination to give a profound sense to all this material, consult Jakob Burckhardt's *The Civilization of the Renais-*

sance in Italy. Burckhardt wrote his book in the 1850s, and historians today like to consider it outdated and mistaken. But for scope, brilliance, and a readiness to reflect deeply on the meaning of it all, Burckhardt puts most of those who have followed him to shame.

Illustration Credits

Page 27: Scala/Art Resource, NY. Uffizi, Florence, Italy. Page 56: Alinari/Art Resource, NY. Baptistery, Florence, Italy. Page 75: Scala/Art Resource, NY. Brancacci Chapel, S. Maria del Carmine, Florence, Italy. Page 102: Scala/Art Resource, NY. Museo Nazionale del Bargello, Florence, Italy. Page 105: Scala/Art Resource, NY. Palazzo Medici Riccardi, Florence, Italy. Page 126: Erich Lessing/Art Resource, NY. Museo di S. Marco, Florence, Italy. Page 129: Erich Lessing/Art Resource, NY. Palazzo Medici Riccardi, Florence, Italy. Page 132: Scala/Art Resource, NY. S. Stefano dei Cavalieri, Pisa, Italy. Page 166: Scala/Art Resource, NY. S. Maria Novella, Florence, Italy. Page 191: Samuel H. Kress Collection, Image © 2004 Board of Trustees, National Gallery of Art, Washington. Page 230: Erich Lessing/Art Resource, NY. Narodowe Museum, Gdansk, Poland. Page 237: Erich Lessing/Art Resource, NY. Museo di S. Marco, Florence, Italy.

Index

Page numbers in *italics* refer to illustrations.